When
Learning
Happens

When Learning Happens

JOHN M. LEMBO

81823

SCHOCKEN BOOKS · NEW YORK

To Anthony, Daniel, and Judy—
my family and favorite teachers

Contents

Preface

DESPITE THE public discussion over the past decade about providing appropriate learning conditions for each student, we have overwhelming evidence that in the average classroom little attention is given to the individual student's interests, ideas, and honest feelings (60, 145).* Instead, within a given class nearly all students are required to engage in the same activities and complete the same tasks at the same rate, and they are subjected to an evaluation system that makes invidious comparisons between students who differ markedly in their learning capabilities. Much of the content that teachers emphasize is trivia, and what they consider important is not in keeping with the reality the learner knows. What is pertinent to a subject is often not shown to be relevant to the learner, nor does the school relate the learner's reality to the process of education.

In too many classrooms teachers are preoccupied with regulations and policies that are designed to control students rather than protect them, and that make learning a degrading experience instead of a joyful one. There is a constant use of threats and punishment to coerce students to perform in ways that are irrelevant to their needs and goals. Each hour students are in school they must be docile, passive, and compliant or run the risk of punishment, failure, or expulsion. Consequently, students find it necessary to spend most of their time in school figuring out what

* Numbers in parentheses refer to bibliographical entries.

the teachers want and devising strategies to deal with the teachers' demands (74, 92).

In short, huge sums of money are wasted each year on "teaching" pupils what they already know or what they don't want or need to know. What most students encounter in most classrooms are irrelevant and nonserviceable curricula, wholly inappropriate teaching strategies, and rules and regulations that contain little logic and have as their corollaries sarcasm, ridicule, threats, and physical abuse. The effects of these procedures are devastating and often irreversible. Many students have experienced all of these conditions in the public schools; and for each such student these conditions over a stretch of years destroy his desire to learn and his ability to think and act as a whole person. He develops feelings of hostility, resentment, and alienation, which occasionally explode into violence. Eventually he may believe that he is incompetent and powerless and needs to remove himself from the school setting (92).

The task before us is one of rebuilding our schools. More specifically, we need to design schools that help our young people to become more open and more sensitive to their environment; to communicate with a minimum of damaging distortion; to develop a view of themselves as competent and productive people; to cope with changing knowledge; to deal effectively with the problems of racial conflict, war, pollution, drug addiction, alienation, crime, and mental illness; to cope with a continually changing code of social ethics and values; to understand their culture and to recognize and perpetuate in a deliberate fashion that which is of value in it. In short, we need to rebuild our schools so that our young people will say, "We want to come here and share our private experiences and join with others to learn about the purpose and nature of man's brief journey, to understand each other's needs and hopes, and to work together to achieve our common goals and solve our common problems."

How can this be done? Innovative practices in a number of classrooms in various parts of our country make it clear that the quality of learning in our schools depends primarily on the kinds of conditions each teacher designs for each of his students. This fact alone suggests that educational reform, if it is to be effective, must center around the classroom teacher. New buildings, new curricula, more money, and more effective administrators may be necessary to make schools physically attractive and operationally sound, but they do not ensure successful learning for each individual. Obviously money and the things it will buy are needed. However, while it takes considerable money to operate schools —to buy materials and equipment, to pay teachers' salaries, and to heat buildings—no amount of money can guarantee reform of the way youngsters learn. We must rely on competent, humane, and resourceful teachers to provide the conditions that enable all students to learn successfully and to live their school years creatively and productively.

It is unlikely that a teacher will automatically develop the competencies to design more effective learning environments simply by reading this book or any book describing classroom strategies that facilitate self-directed learning. No book can be a substitute for effective training and classroom experience in designing and trying out various procedures to discover which ones ensure successful learning. Recent books on informal modes of learning vary in their emphasis of more desirable forms of school organization, more reality-oriented curricula and materials, or more constructive student–teacher relationships. For the average classroom teacher many of these books are inspirational. However, in order for the teacher to help each of his students learn in reasonably satisfying ways, he must be more than inspired. He must be provided with detailed descriptions of techniques and strategies which he can put into effective practice in his own classroom.

I have tried to provide useful information for understanding the nature of the learning process and for designing constructive learning environments. The classroom procedures described are only suggestive of ones that can be used, as each teacher will need to develop his own repertory of teaching skills in his own way to deal with the interacting intellectual, emotional, and social characteristics of the students he finds in his own classroom.

Today the teacher is the crucial link in the educational chain. Two choices are open to him—to remain part of the problem or to become part of the solution. What will the classroom teacher do with this opportunity? Will he use it to perpetuate the ineffective and often destructive practices in our schools? Or will he seize this opportunity to help create shared schools and shared classrooms, and thereby become an instrument of constructive educational change?

It is hoped that he will choose the road less traveled and accept the challenge to design a shared classroom; that he will begin now to help his students become competent and responsible in directing their own learning and in dealing with the entire range of personal and social problems they face.

I wish to express my appreciation to Audrey Burie, Cande O'Donnell, John O'Donnell, and Richard Olds, who carefully read the manuscript and offered a number of valuable suggestions for improving it. I am also deeply indebted to my wife, Judy, who often postponed attention to her own needs to type several drafts of the manuscript.

I wish to thank the following publishers who have granted permission to quote from copyrighted materials: The New American Library for *36 Children,* by Herbert Kohl (copyright © 1967 by Herbert Kohl); Harper & Row, Publishers, for *The Culturally Deprived Child,* by Frank Riessman (copyright © 1962 by Frank Riessman), and *Where, When, and Why,* by Martin Mayer (copyright © 1962, 1963 by Martin Prager Mayer); Scholastic Magazines, Inc., for *Learning Discussion Skills Through Games,* by Gene Stanford and Barbara Dodds Stanford (copyright © 1969 by Scholastic Magazines, Inc.); John Wiley & Sons, Inc., for *Creative Encounters in the Classroom,* by Byron G. Massalias and Jack Zevin (copyright © 1967 by John Wiley & Sons, Inc.); Doubleday & Company for *Teaching for Thinking,* by Thomas G. Aylesworth and Gerald M. Reagan (copyright © 1969 by Doubleday & Company, Inc.; Pitman Publishing Corporation for *Teacher-Pupil Planning for Better Classroom Learning,* by Yvonne Waskin and Louise Parrish (copyright © 1967 by Pitman Publishing Corporation); and Charles E. Merrill for *Why Teachers Fail,* by John M. Lembo (copyright © 1971 by Charles E. Merrill Publishing Co.).

A way must be found to develop, within the educational system as a whole, and in each component, a climate conducive to personal growth, a climate in which the focus is not upon *teaching,* but on the facilitation of *self-directed learning.* Only thus can we develop the creative individual who is open to all of his experience; aware of it and accepting it, and continually in the process of changing.

—CARL ROGERS

I

THE NATURE OF LEARNING

1

The Search for Meaning
and Competence

EVERY MOMENT A person is living he is making discoveries about himself and the world in which he lives. One of his earliest and most important discoveries is that he can make things happen. For example, an infant of eight or nine months discovers that by moving his legs in a certain way he can produce a movement in a set of toy birds suspended over his crib. He discovers that there is a relationship between his behavior and events around him. The same is the case for the older child, the adolescent, and the adult. Each person, regardless of his level of development and maturity, is always discovering that he can make specific things happen by the particular ways in which he acts on his environment.

The developing person also discovers that he has a variety of needs—needs for survival, security, love, and self-esteem, and the need for self-actualization, to develop his unique set of potentials in his own way. Moreover, he discovers that in order to meet these needs he must continually search for ways of dealing competently with his environment. In short, each person discovers not only that he *can* make things happen, but that he *must* make particular kinds of things happen in order to maintain and enhance his life.

Other discoveries that a person makes grow out of his search to find out *why*. He wants to know why some things happen and other things do not happen. For example, a young child may want to know why he is more likely to catch cold in the winter than in the summer, or why leaves fall from some trees but not from others. Each person also wants to know why some things are permitted to happen under some conditions but not under other conditions, and why some things are not permitted to happen at all. For example, a youngster may want to know why he may practice on his drums at ten o'clock in the morning but not at ten o'clock in the evening.

As a result of wanting to know *why,* each person continually makes discoveries about the reasons behind events. The youngster who may not practice on his drums at ten o'clock in the evening discovers that his environment is a shared one and that his efforts to meet his needs often conflict with the efforts of others to meet their needs—that together they must try to meet their individual needs through mutually agreeable means. The developing person, then, not only discovers that he must continually acquire new levels of competence in order to deal effectively with his changing environment, but he also discovers reasons behind events—he continually finds meaning.

An important question for education which grows out of our brief discussion about discoveries is: "How does the search for meaning and competence take place?" That is, "How does learning happen?"

The search for meaning and competence is a continuous process in which the person perceives tentative relationships between himself and his environment, conceptualizes his own ways of finding meaning and interacting competently with his environment, tries out his mental models, and makes judgments about their relevance and effectiveness. The results of the person's learning efforts in turn produce new perceptions about his relationship with his environment and set in motion another cycle of conceptualizing, trying out, and evaluating. These results, in turn, set off another cycle, and so on. Let me try to convey this view of the learning process by describing how a youngster learns through imitation.

The child discovers early that there are both advantages and disadvantages in modeling his behavior after that of his parents.

In many situations he finds that his strategies for achieving goals and satisfying his needs are approved when they are patterned after those of his parents. In other situations he finds, much to his surprise, that when he patterns his strategies after those of his parents, his behavior is disapproved or punished. Consequently, as the result of conceptualizing, trying out, and evaluating a variety of ways of achieving his goals and satisfying his needs in different situations, the child discovers many of the conditions under which he may and may not imitate the behavior of his parents. He discovers as a matter of principle that the behavior his parents display is not always a reliable yardstick for the kinds of behavior they expect of him.

If we were to break the imitation process down into small steps, we might find that the child first observes that his parents possess something he would like to have, e.g., a skill or power. He is thus inclined to believe that if he were to simulate the behavior patterns of his parents, he would be able to secure what he wants. The child then conceptualizes and tries out various strategies to simulate his parents' behavior, looking for cues that indicate he is behaving in the necessary ways. Whenever the child receives information that confirms that his mental model and behavior patterns are helping him to achieve his goal and win the approval of his parents, he continues with his plans and strategies. If he discovers that his ideas and strategies are ineffective or disadvantageous, he makes some modifications in them and tries again to achieve his goals and gain parental approval.

The nature of imitative learning suggests that, regardless of the kind of learning a person engages in—discovering how to read, how to ride a bike, how to solve mathematical problems, or how to be effective in interpersonal transactions—he is continually perceiving relationships, conceptualizing ways of dealing competently with his environment, trying out his mental models, and judging their effectiveness and relevance.

It cannot be overemphasized that the conceptualizing of mental models does not in itself produce reliable discoveries. Even though the learner may conceptualize various answers to questions, various solutions to problems, and various means to an end, he must try out these tentative "discoveries" to determine whether or not they will help him achieve his goals. For example, in imitative learning the person must try out the problem-solving behavior he sees other people employing successfully to determine whether or not this same behavior will be effective for *him*. The trial process itself produces discoveries—discoveries that one's ideas are applicable or inapplicable or in need of modification, that one needs to explore further relationships, that one can use one's behavior effectively only under specific conditions. For example, in imitative learning, the person may discover that he is unsuccessful in his efforts to pattern his behavior after another's because he does not possess all the verbal skills needed to solve his problems. Consequently he may discover that there are specific conditions under which imitative learning will work for him.

The observation that mental models alone are not enough to acquire reliable meanings and competencies is of special significance to education. Too many teachers believe that learning occurs primarily when a student is told the mental models of others— what others believe to be the important relationships and rules in a subject. These same teachers are also inclined to believe that, so long as the student can *retell* the mental models he has been *told,* he has acquired reliable meanings and competencies. For example, many mathematics teachers require a student to listen to and restate geometry theorems or multiplication tables in the belief that the student thereby learns *how* to solve mathematical problems. This form of "conceptualizing," "trying out," and "judging" is one of the lowest forms of human learning, and it certainly does not involve true discovery or the processes of conceptualizing, trying out, and evaluating the relevance and effectiveness of one's *own* ideas. Learning only to associate particular numbers in multiplying does not provide any assurance that the child has learned why particular numbers should be associated, or that the product of associating two particular numbers is a logical one for *him*.

The myth that learning occurs when the teacher tells and the student retells is also evident when students are asked to recite or write the Constitution in the hope that this will produce good citizenship. There is a failure to recognize not only that each student must formulate his own ideas about good citizenship, but that he must also try out his ideas; he must live them to determine their worth. Although information about the nature of good citizenship is useful and advice about upholding our laws is commendable, young people learn to be good citizens only by arriving at conceptions of good citizenship through discussion and debate and by involving themselves in the *activity* of being responsible citizens.

Another example of this myth is found in the beliefs and practices of many teacher trainers. Too many teacher trainers require an education student to tell or write about how to teach effectively after he has been *told* how, in the belief that this is how people learn to teach (92). Teacher trainers need to recognize that in order for a person to become a competent classroom teacher he must not only arrive at his own conceptions of how to teach, but he must also engage in the teaching act itself—trying out his ideas and judging the relevance and effectiveness of his teaching behavior throughout each phase of his education and training.

The preceding discussion on the question of how a person conducts his search for meaning and competence suggests to the teacher that his students cannot conduct a true search if he designs a classroom in which the acts of teacher-telling and student-retelling become substitutes for the student's formulating, trying out, and evaluating. Regardless of the meanings and competencies sought, a person will not make reliable discoveries unless he conducts each phase of the discovery process himself and in his own way.

Another important point about the search for meaning and competence is that a student always discovers more than the teacher intends. A student does not acquire a skill such as swimming without also acquiring some knowledge, feelings, and attitudes about swimming and about himself. The student, for example, acquires knowledge about coordination and limits of endurance, and he develops feelings and attitudes such as whether or not swimming is an enjoyable activity, or a good means of developing positive relationships with others.

The student learning to solve problems in a physics class by the scientific method is, to be sure, learning about the nature of the scientific method and how to use it, but he is also learning the language of physics. And he is learning who he is and what his capabilities are from the ways in which he is treated by those who interact with him as he tries to solve physics problems.

The girl who is learning how to take shorthand is learning many arbitrary relationships between words and visual symbols and how to form and apply the symbols. However, she is at the same time forming attitudes toward shorthand, toward her teachers, toward the business world, and toward herself.

In the classroom, then, each student discovers not only many of the meanings, rules, and skills of a subject, but also the kind of place the classroom is, the kind of person the teacher is, and the kind of person he himself is or can become (33).

Moreover, the different kinds of discoveries that a person makes are interdependent. We know, for example, that unless a student discovers how to deal with psychological stress he will have considerable difficulty reasoning in logical ways and being creative. We also know that when an individual is repeatedly unable to find answers, to achieve goals, and to solve problems in the classroom, he is not likely to develop a positive feeling about himself—a feeling that he is competent, that he has worth. This point, and the observation that the student always learns more than a field of study, suggest that the student always conducts his search for meaning and competence as a whole person (92). The student's perceptions of his world, his present skills and concerns, and his feelings toward himself and others continually and simultaneously interact as he attempts to find answers, solve problems, and achieve goals. The implication of this observation is that one of the teacher's primary responsibilities in the classroom is to help each student develop *all* of his capabilities for perceiving, thinking, feeling, and doing, and develop them in an integrated fashion in each area of study.

The teacher must not make the mistake of promoting the development of one set of competencies to the exclusion of others or of attending to one set of psychological needs and ignoring others. When a teacher denies a student the opportunity to develop fully, the student may learn highly disadvantageous ways of dealing with his environment. For example, if a teacher chooses to promote intellectual development alone, he runs the risk of teaching the student that feelings and emotions should not be taken into account when attempting to resolve issues. Or if the teacher chooses to promote only emotional development, he runs the risk of teaching the student that logic and the scientific method have no place in the problem-solving and decision-making processes. In short, he fragments the student's search for meaning and competence, and denies the student the opportunity to develop *all* the skills he needs to deal with all the different kinds of human questions and problems he encounters inside and outside the classroom. Classrooms must not be centers for intellectual development alone or for emotional development alone, but for *human* development (27, 92). In each classroom, whether the subject be mathematics, English, physics, or history, the teacher must relate the field of study to all of the student's feelings and ideas about himself and his world.

To summarize: whether we examine the lives of children, youths, or adults, we find that each person is always searching for meaning and competence. His discoveries evolve out of his behavior within his environment and his interpretation of how the environment responds to that behavior. He actively conceptualizes his own mental models for interacting competently with his environment, tries out these models, and checks their relevance and effectiveness for answering questions, solving problems, and achieving goals. Further, the student's search for meaning and competence is a search by the whole person, involving his perceptions, knowledge, feelings, attitudes, values, and skills in an integrated fashion.

2

One's Own Way

EVERY TEACHER HAS his own beliefs about why students learn some things and not others, and many teachers believe that unless students are pressed into particular behavior patterns they will not develop in ways that are advantageous to themselves and others. Yet observations indicate that each individual, to deal competently with his environment, has a basic need to explore, to know, to find meaning in reality, and to develop necessary skills. He does not have to be coerced to learn and develop in constructive ways. Each person is always learning, and he always *wants* to learn.

The infant continually explores his environment and attempts to reach objects, to touch, to feel what he sees, to search for meanings, to make things happen. The toddler picks up a cup, puts his hand in it, takes it out, puts blocks into the cup, dumps them out, and so on, trying to discover the different things he can do with it. Playing in the soft mud, he will push and pull his foot or hand through it to hear the sounds it makes and to experience how it feels. He forms mud into objects and symbols and puts it in his mouth to discover its taste. In the sandbox he lets a handful of sand trickle between his fingers, or he pours it from one container to another, or plunges his hands and arms into a pile of sand up to his shoulders, discovering what he can do with it and what it means to him. He engages in these activities because he *wants* to discover (84, 118, 119).

He begins early to gather data about his world and the effects his behavior has on it. He begins early to store information about cause-and-effect relationships—that when he does one thing another thing happens. He begins to identify events and objects in his world with sounds people make and with written symbols, and he develops a repertory of such sounds and symbols to describe relationships between himself and his world. He gradually extends his skills through his use of sounds and symbols, discovering that he can predict and control many aspects of his behavior and his environment (84). He learns to behave in these ways *naturally,* because he has questions, wants answers, and wants to be competent.

As the child develops, he continually refines his strategies for discovering. He tends to search for specific results, performing orderly transactions with the different aspects of his physical and social environment, to discover systematic relationships between his acts and those of things, animals, and other people. He becomes concerned not only with finding out "why" and "how" but with forming reliable rules about his behavior and about events in his environment—rules which he in turn can use to predict and control a large number of events and to seek solutions and answers to his concerns (84). He does all of these things without coercion.

When we examine the behavior of older children, we find that, regardless of their background, they, too, immerse themselves in constructive activities without any prodding, sometimes discovering far more than we would predict. For example, we see how much a youngster discovers when he sets out to care for a puppy or a rabbit, to plant his own garden, to collect insects, leaves, and rocks, or to build a soapbox racer, a radio, or a tree house. Although few of the conditions are present that we like to think are essential for acquiring useful skills, a youngster often learns more on his own than when he attacks some of our well-planned classroom problems. More often than not, a youngster reads instructions that are beyond his "reading level" in school, and he gathers information on his own from many sources. There is no need for his parents to force him to learn; nor do they need to maintain a "record of attendance" or threaten him with examinations to keep him involved with his activity. He explores, discovers, and completes useful, skill-developing activities without any rigid class-room structure or any formal instruction. The youngster learns simply because he wants to know. He wants to do things. He wants to answer questions, solve problems, and achieve goals. He is always motivated to discover (84, 150).

The classroom teacher may be prompted by this discussion to ask: "If a youngster is always motivated to learn, why then in our modern, clean, well-organized, well-heated, well-lighted, and well-equipped classrooms do I need to force this same youngster to learn?" More specifically, the question is: Why does a teacher find it difficult to teach a youngster to complete in-class activities that appear far simpler than the out-of-class activities he handles with ease? For example, why is a youngster who must collect money for newspapers able to learn to make change correctly, and yet is unable to grasp many of the fundamentals in mathe-matics? Why does he find it easy to remember the exact sequence of cartoons and adventure programs playing on television, when he is unable to recall a single line of poetry? Why should he have little difficulty discovering how to travel from one part of a large city to another and yet encounter extreme difficulty in learning to follow the simplest directions for completing a homework as-signment? Our knowledge of human behavior tells us that a person learns certain things, many of which are complex, yet appears unable to learn other things, many of which are simple, because he searches for, discovers, and achieves that which he perceives to be important to his present and immediate needs and purposes.

For each learner, it is first of all a here-and-now world for discovery (33). Although it is valuable for a youngster to discover how major economic, political, social, and cultural events have developed historically, and although he must eventually come to grips with a number of questions in the distant future, the young-ster's motives for learning are those he has *now*. Since a youngster lives only in the present, he will learn about the past or prepare for the future only if his learning builds on what he values *now*.

There is another reason why a youngster learns some things and not others: not only is it impossible for him to value the past, present, and future equally, but he cannot perceive or value everything that is in the present equally. Out of the thousands of possible transactions he can engage in at a given point in time, he intentionally or unintentionally selects specific transactions, and he acquires specific meanings and skills in each transaction and carries these on to subsequent transactions. Discovering is not only a here-and-now process, it is a self-selection process for each individual (25).

Each individual in each classroom has a unique set of needs: his own questions, his own fears, his own interests, his own ambitions—all of which are integrated to direct his behavior at a given point in time. Often these needs are served in terms of priorities, with some needs more important to the person than others. For one individual, his most important current need is a set of questions he wants answered. For a second individual, it may also be a set of questions, but a different set. For another individual, it may be a need to feel liked and accepted. And for yet another, the most important need may be to feel safe from physical or psychological threats. Consequently, each individual will select what he wants to discover at a given point because of the way he sees his own particular set of needs.

This makes it quite clear that providing opportunities for discovery in no way guarantees that particular kinds of discoveries will occur. When a student sits in a classroom exposed to what the teacher is presenting, he will discover only that which has meaning for *him*. He will make selections based on his perceptions of his current needs, his perception of classroom life, and his current perceptions of himself as a person.

He is in his own way continually engaged in learning for ends and purposes that he believes are worthwhile to *him*. He pursues what he believes to be personally valuable, and he retains and integrates those selections that he believes are usable now and will have increasing value for him in the future. He does not pursue what he believes to be irrelevant to his current needs and purposes. If the teacher asks a student to discover or attend to something that he views as unimportant to his current life, the student will generally oblige, to see where the teacher is taking him. However, unless *his* questions are answered, *his* fears handled, and *his* concerns examined, the student may not indulge the teacher very long (92).

The teacher will also discover that a student cannot be made to "learn" something he does not want to learn. In fact, the student will demonstrate considerable ingenuity in devising the coping and surviving strategies needed to avoid and escape what are for him contrived and meaningless learning activities. He will cut classes, feign illnesses, "underachieve," lie, daydream, cheat, and openly resist. "Nothing else can be expected when the student is legitimately concerned about his own needs and questions, and the teacher chooses to ignore or reject them" (92).

Learning according to one's current needs has another important aspect. Learning is more than selecting and pursuing that which provides continuity in one's life; it is expressing one's own rhythm or rate of searching and discovering. When we observe the individual learner, we find that he does not learn in predictable amounts each day or week (61). On the contrary, he may become intensely involved in discovery, level off in his rate of activity, decline briefly, and then forge ahead again. The patterns are endlessly variable. Different concerns, goals, and needs may arise and may suddenly cease. On some days he does not show much interest, and on other days he finds himself digging in and grappling with problems. On some days he makes only partial discoveries, with many relationships between particular events remaining to be discovered later. On other days he discovers all of the details or all of the steps for achieving a goal. On some days his discoveries occur quickly because a particular problem, issue, or situation is familiar or the ideas and behavior involved are apparent to him. On other days his discoveries occur slowly because the situation, problem, or issue, or the ideas and behavior involved, are so unfamiliar to him that he needs to explore, conceptualize, and try out ideas, and evaluate the effects of his behavior several times before he can accumulate enough information and skill to deal satisfactorily with the problem in question.

Nor does a learner progress "all of a piece"; he tends to discover more rapidly in some areas than in others. For example, "Johnny can be in the fifth grade for arithmetic computation, the sixth grade for arithmetic reasoning, the seventh for spelling, the eighth for word meaning, the ninth for paragraph meaning and the tenth for language—and yet be officially registered in the sixth grade" (59). Moreover, the differences in a student's rates of learning in different areas may increase with the passage of time; a small difference observed in a seven-year-old's rates of learning about wild animals and sports may extend to a sizable difference by the time he is fourteen or fifteen, when athletics become very important for achieving group status.

When we look at youngsters' behavior we also find that each has his own style of learning. One youngster may prefer to pursue his interests through reading; another may prefer to listen to people describe events and explain how to do something; others may prefer to try out something through using their hands or through representing their ideas with physical structures; and still others prefer to talk through their ideas with others. Some youngsters are easily discouraged and need continual support to commit themselves to a goal for a lengthy period of time; they need to be provided with a schedule to complete the selected activities. Other youngsters are capable of committing themselves to specific goals and completing the activity successfully without reassurance or reminders from an adult. Some youngsters enjoy being helped by older and brighter youngsters; others prefer to be in situations in which they do the helping. Some youngsters learn best from an adult teacher; others learn best when they are taught by their peers. Some youngsters prefer to work alone; others prefer to work in a group. Some youngsters prefer to walk about at a leisurely pace while they read; some prefer to stretch out while reading; still others prefer to sit at a desk. Some prefer background music while reading, solving a problem, or constructing something; others prefer silence while they work. Some youngsters grasp an idea all at once or in large pieces; others need to have each idea broken down into very small parts. Some young-sters require direct experiences or firsthand encounters to acquire reliable meanings about events; others do their best learning with films, books, maps, slides, and tapes. Some youngsters need short assignments that give them frequent feelings of accomplishment; they are overwhelmed by long, complex tasks or a long learning contract (see Chapter 7). Other youngsters prefer long tasks or learning contracts so they can make their own plans and set their own pace. Some youngsters need to receive both continuous feed-back about their progress and detailed suggestions in order to achieve their goals; others need only occasional feedback and very few suggestions (91, 133).

All of these observations suggest not only that the learning process is shaped by the unique needs, skills, concerns, and learning style of the student, but also that the learning process shapes each student into a unique individual. That is to say, as each developing student forms his own perceptions of himself and his environment and acquires his own meanings and skills at his own rate and in his own way, he creates a unique basis for each sequence of meaning-producing and skill-developing expe-riences that are appropriate for him. The new experiences that may be most effective in providing continuity in his life at any given point in time may not be equally effective in providing continuity in the life of any other student at the same point in time. Consequently, as the developing student is styling the learn-ing process in a unique way for himself, the learning process is at the same time shaping the developing student into a unique person.

That each student conducts his search for meaning and com-petence in a unique way is the single most important principle the teacher needs to keep in mind when organizing a classroom. No single set of objectives, no single set of materials or activities, no single period of time is appropriate for all students to learn and develop optimally. No single method of grouping students—whether by age, sex, size, achievement, test scores, or IQ—is capable of dealing with all of the important learning character-istics each student brings to a classroom activity. No single organizational procedure, including the "open-space" approach, can ensure the necessary attention to students' different rates and styles of learning. This last point is especially important in view of the increasing susceptibility of many educators to the magical thinking that, if they replace a "closed" structure with an "open" one, each student will automatically do his best learning—as if an organizational structure alone were the necessary and sufficient condition for optimal learning. An organizational structure is advantageous to students only when it deals adequately with their different rates and styles of learning. Consequently, an open structure may be just as ineffective for facilitating learning as other structures. We know, for example, that some students who come from traditional classrooms with thirty or thirty-five students often feel lost or afraid, or find that there are too many distractions, when they are thrust immediately into an open-space structure with 100 or 150 students. Unless they are given a chance to pass through a number of transitional phases—unless they have a chance to learn first in small groups, then in increasingly larger groups—the open-space approach may impede rather than facilitate learning. Therefore, while some features of an open structure, such as independent study, self-selected groups, random learning, and "student-as-teacher," may be highly effective approaches for some students, they may not be appropriate for other students. Several features of the traditional approach, such as regular classroom meetings, sequential learning, and "adult-as-teacher," are essential to help many students do their best learning.

Understanding that the learning process is highly personal for each student, and recognizing that no single organizational structure or set of activities, materials, or objectives automatically takes into account each student's learning characteristics, the teacher needs to address himself to this question: "How can I arrange conditions in my classroom so that each student's concerns, skills, and rate and style of learning receive adequate attention?" More specifically, "How can I teach so that each student finds learning natural rather than forced; so that each student finds continuity rather than segmentation in his learning; so that each student finds his knowledge and skills integrated rather than compartmentalized; so that each student sees himself as the instrument of his own development rather than as an instrument for fulfilling the demands and wishes of others; so that each student sees himself as a competent and worthy person rather than as a failure?"

When we consider the course of natural learning, i.e., that each student conducts his search for meaning and competence in his own way and in terms of his particular set of immediate needs and concerns, we find that the teacher is faced with three fundamental responsibilities. He needs to (*1*) prize each student for himself, (*2*) meet each student where he is, and (*3*) build in each student the freedom and commitment he needs to manage his own learning successfully. The next section will discuss these three responsibilities and describe how the effective teacher would meet them to facilitate personally meaningful and socially constructive learning in each student.

II

THE TEACHER'S BEHAVIOR

3

Prizing Each Student for Himself

THE BELIEFS THAT the developing child acquires about himself are shaped by the evaluations significant persons in his life make of his behavior. That is to say, more often than not a person evaluates himself in the same way he believes "significant others" evaluate him. Thus, acceptance by people who are important in a person's life is instrumental in building self-acceptance, and rejection by these people cultivates self-rejection.

The self-image that a person thus develops influences in turn his behavior and learning. The belief he develops about his ability to perform and discover, for example, influences the kinds of activities and tasks he will seek and the rate of searching and discovering he will display. A person who learns to see himself as being accepted and competent, as having valuable skills, will be more committed, enthusiastic, and successful in his pursuits than a person who does not learn to see himself in this way.

In fact, what a person believes about himself as a learner may be far more important in influencing his rate of discovering than is his IQ or the difficulty of the subject. Many children are unable to read because they see themselves as "poor readers" or "nonreaders." They have learned from the ineffective guidance and the negative and demeaning evaluations of teachers that they are people who cannot read. Similar "learning problems" in other subjects can be traced to children's ideas of themselves as being unable to spell, unable to write, unable to do algebra, or whatever. A. W. Combs points out the circular process in the child who believes he cannot read (24):

> Such a child is likely to avoid reading, and thus the very experience which might change his concept of self is bypassed. Worse still, the child who believes himself unable to read, confronted with the necessity for reading, is more likely than not to do badly. The external evaluation of his teachers and fellow pupils, as well as his own observations of his performance, all provide proof to the child of how right he was in the first place! The possession of a particular concept of self tends to produce behavior that corroborates the self-concept with which the behavior originated. [P. 667]

The student who is treated and consequently comes to view himself as slow, careless, mischievous, or lazy will behave accordingly and will not give himself a chance to learn otherwise. Moreover, until he is presented with convincing evidence that he is valued or until he is treated as a person who has valuable skills, he will continue to believe that he is not very competent or worthy. Research on this self-fulfilling prophecy in recent years suggests that (1) the beliefs a student has about himself determine the extent to which he will engage in skill-developing activities; (2) both the student's beliefs about himself and the extent to which he engages in skill-developing activities are directly related to the ways he is treated and evaluated by the people with whom he interacts for extended periods of time; and (3) negative evaluations of a student's school performance, coupled with inappropriate teaching strategies, often shape in the student a self-concept of inadequacy and defeat (58, 138, 139).

What can the teacher do to help each student develop a positive view of himself? To ensure the development of a positive self-concept as well as to incite motivation to learn and facilitate the acquisition of effective learning skills in each student, the teacher must prize each student as a worthy person—as having competencies and value *as he is*. Perhaps the three most effective ways in which the teacher can demonstrate that he prizes a student are accepting the student on his own terms, listening with empathy to the student's feelings and meanings, and being honest and real with the student in each interpersonal transaction (25, 92, 135).

Accepting Each Student on His Own Terms

To accept a person as he is, is to accept his feelings, his language, his ideas, his experience, and his background. It is to accept him when he is apathetic and when he is enthusiastic, when he is selfish and when he is sharing. It is to accept his strategies for solving problems, his ways of being affectionate and appreciative, his anger with authority. It is to understand his logic for doing what he does. It is to accept his ambitions, his hopes, his expectations. It is to accept his joy when his hopes have been realized or when he achieves a challenging goal. It is to accept his disappointment, anger, frustration, sadness, and depression when he does not achieve a goal or complete an activity in the way he had hoped. When a teacher accepts a student, he is saying to him, "Your ideas and feelings are important to me and I view you as a good and worthwhile person."

When a teacher communicates to a student that he believes the student is competent, the student eventually begins to believe the teacher and to behave in these terms. He believes that his ideas and feelings *do* have merit. He allows himself to explore more about himself and his environment, to present tentative answers, to advance proposals to solve problems. He is open to the development of new ideas, feelings, and behavior. He is not afraid to make mistakes. A student who is made to feel acceptable as he is, never views himself as a failure and never stops searching for meaning and competence.

It is easy, of course, for a teacher to value the student whose learning patterns make few, if any, demands on him or whose background and views are similar to his. However, a highly active student, a student who is constantly exploring and asking questions, or a student whose learning style requires the teacher to make significant changes in his teaching behavior is frequently threatening or irritating. More often than not, a teacher behaves toward an active and inquiring student in ways that reduce the student's activeness and dampen his exploratory behavior. Such a teacher fails to recognize that when he employs techniques to suppress the student's particular style of finding meaning, the student will come to feel that his behavior is unacceptable and in turn suspect that he may be unacceptable as a person. If the teacher is to help each student become a competent learner and see himself as a worthy person, he must accept the student's particular approach to finding meaning and acquiring skills.

If the teacher would like to discover how understanding he is of the feelings and ideas of others, the following experiment may help to provide some insight into his own attitudes and behavior (122). Conduct a class discussion on a controversial topic. After the class, take a sheet of paper and draw a vertical line down the center of it, dividing it into two columns, a "positive" column and a "negative" column. Next select the name of a student who actively participated in the discussion and write in the appropriate column the positive and negative qualities that you believe characterize him. Now ask yourself why you perceive the student the way you do. Check the number of times you wrote down value-laden terms such as *good, bad, right, wrong, intelligent, dull.* Why do you believe you chose these terms? Ask yourself to what extent your approval or disapproval, acceptance or rejection, of the student's behavior is based on your need to use your own personality as a model of acceptable student behavior. Do you generally have positive perceptions of him when his attitudes and behavior are similar to yours? The basic question is: "Do you believe you are capable of seeing each student as unique —as entitled to his *own* ideas, feelings, and values?"

If you find it extremely difficult to perceive the reality that the student sees and to appreciate his views and feelings, then it may be equally difficult for you to help him plan classroom activities that will be personally meaningful to him.

Listening with Empathy

In order to accept a student as he is and thereby prize him, the teacher must understand what the student is feeling and thinking. Consequently, the teacher must be concerned not so much with the student's words or actions, but with the meanings and feelings lying behind his language and behavior. For example, instead of viewing a student's question in terms of *logical* meanings—e.g., "Is that question relevant?"—the teacher should view his question in terms of *psychological* meanings, by asking himself, "What is the student perceiving in this situation that makes this question important for him?"

The teacher may discover that many students are at first unable to communicate their true feelings, either because they don't understand them or because they are afraid to disclose them. For example, when a student is afraid of being punished for his feelings of anger, he may deny his true feelings or accuse others of harboring similar feelings in an effort to turn the spotlight away from himself. Students employ these and many other kinds of defense mechanisms, sometimes simultaneously, to reduce the painful feelings they are experiencing and/or to avoid disclosing their true feelings. Consequently, the teacher's task of discovering a student's true feelings is often difficult. Moreover, with thirty or more students in the classroom and with the rapidity with which interpersonal transactions take place, it is not possible to acquire a comprehensive understanding of each student's concerns and feelings. However, empathic listening—perhaps the most important condition for understanding—can be provided by every teacher. The teacher may never know many of the complex factors lying behind the student's motivation and behavior, but he can listen to what the child is currently communicating and thereby improve the likelihood that the student will feel accepted and valued as a person (135).

A suggestion that may help a teacher improve his skills for accurate and sensitive listening has been offered by Carl Rogers (136). Conduct a class discussion on a controversial topic and state that each member of the class may freely state his own attitudes and feelings on the issue, with one condition: before anyone may express his own personal views or make a statement, he must restate the meanings that the preceding speaker communicated, and he must restate them to the satisfaction of that speaker. This experiment requires each class member, including the teacher, to look at his own ability to listen accurately to every other member of the class, and it reveals to him whether or not he is willing and able to listen to the individual meanings of each class member.

Being Real

Another specific teacher behavior that creates a climate for feeling prized is being real, honest, and constructive in all exchanges of ideas and feelings. When the teacher is a real person who shares his experiences with the student, the student is likely to be real and to share his experiences with the teacher. When the teacher reveals who he is as a person, what he thinks, how he feels, where he spent his childhood, what adventures he had, and what he wants to do most with his life, his students are inclined to believe that he has confidence in them, that he sees them as important people, that he *accepts* them.

Realness between teacher and student is needed to encourage the development of realistic perceptions in the classroom. Students must learn that teachers too are human, that they have needs, problems, and concerns that are just as important as those of the students. A teacher who is real is better able to communicate to the student that, on the one hand, he can disagree with the student's ideas or behavior and that, on the other hand, he views the student as a worthy person. Realness along with sensitive listening enables the teacher to understand more of the dynamics behind a student's interests and boredom, joy and sadness, fears and hopes.

There will be times when the teacher will be unable to prize a student—unable to accept his ideas, to listen empathically, to be honest with him. There will be times when the teacher will be distrustful of a student, when he will resent his behavior, when he will be judgmental and critical in his statements. There will be times when his students will distrust *him,* when they will find *his* views unacceptable. There will be times when the teacher and students will be angry and frustrated with each other. This is the nature of open and honest classroom life (135).

It must be pointed out, however, that these are delicate psychological situations, placing a special obligation on the teacher to be constructive in his interactions with students. On the one hand, the teacher and students are entitled to be angry, frustrated, impatient, and distrustful and to let each other know how they feel in the classroom. It is precisely when the teacher and his students are responding in these ways, when they are open and real—clearly aware of each other's feelings and views and able to state them "just as they are within themselves"—that the teacher and students will find they can begin to accept each other in the classroom and plan and implement more productive learning programs (135). It is only when the teacher and students emerge as real people in the classroom that a free environment based on respect and trust will evolve. On the other hand, the teacher has the responsibility for creating a psychologically safe classroom environment that ensures freedom of expression and constructive interpersonal transactions. Under no condition can the teacher justify destructive behavior on his part or on the part of his students.

One useful guide to help the teacher be real and constructively honest is for him to describe how he feels about the student's behavior rather than to make value judgments about the student as a person (64, 136). The constructive teacher might say, "This persistent loud talking is making me angry; now what do you think we can do about it?" This approach maintains respect for the student as a person, while recognizing his need to know the effect his behavior is having on the teacher. When the student appreciates the effect of his behavior, constructive change can occur. The appropriate outcome may be for the student to modify some aspect of his behavior, or it may be that he can explain to the teacher something about his behavior that will change the teacher's feelings.

Some teachers, unfortunately, find that they cannot be real or honest with students without being destructive, or that they are unable to modify their behavior in ways that facilitate learning. They discover that they cannot recognize and express their feelings toward each student but can only make value judgments about him. They discover that they cannot find good things in a student's behavior and communicate them to him with words such as "That's good," "You are improving," "You're doing fine." Often such a teacher tries to deny or submerge his negative feelings toward students. However, if a teacher says positive things about a student's behavior while having negative feelings toward him, the student will eventually find the teacher out. The student may not know exactly what the teacher is really thinking or feeling, but he will know there is something wrong, and he will be reluctant to be real and honest in his response. Such a teacher cannot hope to have students believe for any length of time that he prizes them. What is the teacher to do if he discovers that he cannot be real and constructively honest with each student and cannot accept him as he is? Although few questions in education have simple answers, I believe this question is one that does: if the teacher finds that he must be phony or deceptive in his transactions with a student in order to have him believe he is valued, the teacher has no business being in a classroom!

A teacher considering establishing a real relationship with his students may well ask, "Won't students take advantage of me, or use me, or run all over me if I am truly open and real with them?" I believe that the teacher need not worry about "losing control" of his class when he prizes his students. Prizing is not being sentimental, and being real does not exclude the use of rules to govern interpersonal behavior. When the teacher prizes a student, he is saying, "I understand, I can see why you feel this way and why you want to do this." However, while a teacher can appreciate the student's views, feelings, and the reasons he gives for wanting to do something, the teacher is still free to take issue with the student's behavior, and, if necessary, to intervene in interpersonal conflicts.

The right to express one's feelings and the right to be free of psychological and physical abuse are sacred to the teacher as well as to the student. Further, the teacher must be viewed as having the authority to prevent disorder and destruction. However, when he finds it necessary to intervene in destructive interpersonal relationships, he cannot simply censure the student. He must convey to the student that he is valued and wanted, while at the same time making clear to him the destructiveness of his approach. Alternative behavior patterns that the student is capable of exhibiting must be identified, and those that are acceptable to both the student and teacher must be encouraged and supported. This amounts to helping the student discover more about the consequences of his behavior while at the same time helping him retain the belief that he is prized as a person.

In summary, learning to believe in oneself does not occur in a vacuum; a student learns that he is worthy in the classroom primarily by being prized by his teacher. If the teacher does not value the student, he makes it impossible for the student to value himself. The student who believes he is not valued is almost always trying to find value in his behavior by defending or justifying it. He will lie, devise excuses, and engage in whatever behavior he believes is needed to try to protect himself from being viewed as worthless. If the teacher hopes to have each student be a highly motivated and successful learner, he must view the student's offerings as valuable contributions and he must continually search for effective ways of communicating to the student that he prizes him. The teacher can do this by listening empathically to the feelings and meanings the student is trying to communicate and by being real and constructively honest in his transactions with the student. Being real means that the teacher also has feelings and that he has the right to demand and expect constructive behavior from his students.

4

Meeting the Student Where He Is

IF THE TEACHER prizes each student as he is, then it follows inexorably that the teacher must make teaching decisions in terms of the student's current knowledge, skills, concerns, and rate and style of learning. The teacher who does not make decisions in this way is in effect saying to the student, "I don't care who you are and I don't place any value on what you bring to this classroom." However, if the teacher is to have each student learn willingly and satisfactorily, he has no choice but to have the individual learning characteristics the student brings to the classroom dictate the learning conditions the teacher arranges for him (59).

I know it has become a cliché in education to say to the teacher, "You must begin where the student is"; however, the truth is as obvious and relevant in this cliché as in the metaphor about the horse led to water. Just as it is true that you can lead a horse to water, but the only water that gets into his stomach is what he chooses to drink, so it is true that a person will learn only in terms of the way he perceives his needs and purposes. Admittedly, all of us have "learned" some things we weren't vitally interested in, and we only discovered what we had learned much later when a need relevant to the learning arose. However, teachers must realize that each student can and may psychologically "veto" any classroom activity or event he cannot relate to his current skills and perceptions of himself and his world.

Unfortunately, very little in our schools is oriented toward the student's current ideas, skills, or concerns. Virtually all activities and materials arise out of abstractions and concerns that are future- or past-oriented. Although each student lives in a world of primary, face-to-face encounters, he is required to engage in activities, such as learning calculus or a foreign language, that he believes have little relationship to his current life. The student is being taught for a future that does not and perhaps cannot impress itself upon him; hence, he sees little need to focus his energies upon learning for the hypothetical future. Moreover, students feel uncertain about which skills will be relevant to an uncertain future. This is true for students at all economic levels. They all realize they will need many new and different skills in the future, but this realization provides neither any motivation for the present nor any accurate description of the specific skills and knowledge applicable to that future (39).

Moreover, while many of the skills each student must acquire to deal effectively with the future are those needed to work creatively with symbols and abstractions, the acquisition of these skills cannot be either the starting point in learning or the core of learning. The teacher needs to begin with the concrete experiences that the students are having or have had outside the classroom, and he needs to help them build abstractions and the skills to work with these abstractions through their concrete experiences. Without such an approach, symbols, abstractions, and the skills to work with them lose both their connection with the learner's current life and their capacity to be useful to him in the future. Teaching abstractions and symbols through students' current experiences is precisely what Herbert Kohl did with his thirty-six children (88). For example, he recalls the following incident:

> One day Ralph cursed at Michael and unexpectedly things came together for me. Michael was reading and stumbled several times. Ralph scornfully called out, "What's the matter, psyches, going to pieces again?" The class broke up and I jumped on that word "psyches."

"Ralph, what does *psyches* mean?"

An embarrassed silence.

"Do you know how to spell it?"

Alvin volunteered. "S-i-k-e-s."

"Where do you think the word came from? Why did everybody laugh when you said it, Ralph?"

"You know, Mr. Kohl, it means, like crazy or something."

"Why? How do words get to mean what they do?"

Samuel looked up at me and said: "Mr. Kohl, now you're asking questions like Alvin. There aren't any answers, you know that."

"But there are. Sometimes by asking Alvin's kind of questions you discover the most unexpected things. Look."

I wrote *Psyche,* then *Cupid,* on the blackboard. "That's how *psyche* is spelled. It looks strange in English, but the word doesn't come from English. It's Greek. There's a letter in the Greek alphabet that comes out *psi* in English. This is the way *psyche* looks in Greek.

"The word *psyche* has a long history. *Psyche* means mind or soul for the Greeks, but it was also the name of a lovely woman who had the misfortune to fall in love with Cupid, the son of Venus, the jealous Greek goddess of love. . . ."

The children listened, enchanted by the myth, fascinated by the weaving of the meaning of *psyche* into the fabric of the story, and the character, *Mind,* playing tricks on itself, almost destroying its most valuable possessions through its perverse curiosity. . . .

I cited *psychological, psychic, psychotic, psychodrama, cupidity*—the children copied them unasked, demanded the meanings. They were obviously excited.

Leaping ahead, Alvin shouted: "You mean words change? People didn't always speak this way? Then how come the reader says there's a right way to talk and a wrong way?"

"There's a right way now, and that only means that's how most people would like to talk now, and how people write now."

Charles jumped out of his desk and spoke for the first time during the year.

"You mean one day the way we talk—you know, with words like *cool* and *dig* and *sound*—may be all right?"

"Uh huh. Language is alive, it's always changing, only some-

times it changes so slowly that we can't tell." Neomia caught on.
"Mr. Kohl, is that why our reader sounds so old-fashioned?"
And Ralph.

"Mr. Kohl, when I called Michael *psyches,* was I creating
something new?"

Someone spoke for the whole class.

"Mr. Kohl, can't we study the language we're talking about
instead of spelling and grammar? They won't be any good when
language changes anyway."

We could and did. That day we began what had to be called
for my conservative plan book "vocabulary," and "an enrichment
activity. . . ." They found it easy to master and acquire words
that would have seemed senseless and tedious to memorize. Words
like *psychic* and *psychosomatic* didn't seem arbitrary and im-
penetrable, capable of being learned only painfully by rote. Rather
they existed in a context, through a striking tale that easily accrued
associations and depth. After a week the children learned the new
words, asked to be tested on them, and demanded more. [Pp.
33–35]

Kohl began with the children's language and meanings to plan
learning activities. As a result he was successful in developing
high levels of motivation in his students and in helping them to
improve their reading and self-expression and to acquire some of
the important abstractions and symbols needed to understand
some of the relationships in their social environment.

The advantages of starting where the student is are most clearly
recognized in the acquisition of necessary skills and in the enhance-
ment of motivation. With regard to acquiring skills, a student
cannot learn a complex skill if he has not mastered its prerequisites
or component parts. For example, a student cannot do long division unless he is able to add, subtract, multiply, and divide and
unless he understands place value. The only mathematics he will
learn will depend on his current knowledge and skills and not on
the teacher's expectations or demands. With regard to motivation,
a student will persist and succeed in achieving specific goals only
when the goals reflect his current capabilities and concerns. While
success in the past and an expectation of success in the future are

essential for a student to be highly motivated in a new activity, high motivation and success are ensured only when the goals and activities are consonant with the learner's concerns and capabilities. When the teacher starts where the learner is, motivation to learn is inherent in the learning program, and the probability of successful learning is quite high; the student thrusts himself into activities and encounters, and with each small success he becomes more willing and able to complete advanced activities.

In addition to describing some of the advantages of starting where the student is, it is also important to note briefly some of the possible disadvantages of *not* starting where he is.

To expect or demand a student to begin where he is not, to progress at a rate and in a manner other than his own, and to pursue goals and engage in activities established by others is to risk failure, alienation, and psychological damage. For too long, schools have tried to train youngsters with different ideas, feelings, and concerns to think and behave in the same way and at the same rate. Not only have the schools been unsuccessful in their efforts, but they have helped to produce a culture of youngsters who are lonely, hostile, emotionally twisted, and disadvantaged in many problem-solving skills.

Admittedly, it is desirable to expect students to achieve high standards if they can and want to achieve them. However, when schools require students to achieve standards unrelated to their goals and capabilities, students only learn to view themselves as failures, even when they have tried to do their best. *When the teacher utilizes high but irrelevant standards to prod a student to "get ahead," there is often a very real danger that he will teach the student that he is never acceptable as he is.*

A person feels that he is important, able, worthy, and successful when he can solve important and challenging problems. However, teachers often fail to recognize that what is important and challenging to a teacher may not be important and challenging to the student. Too often, the teacher develops classroom activities and employs "motivating" techniques only because of the value they hold for him, rather than for the effects they have on the student. This approach, coupled with the teacher's demand that each student progress at the same rate and in the same way, inevitably leads the student to believe that he continually needs the direction of others, that he is unable to discover by himself what he wants to do with his life and how he can succeed.

Although one of the major concerns of education is to produce "competence," a failure to view competence as an *individual* achievement—as relative to the individual student's capabilities—produces precisely the opposite. When classroom objectives and experiences are unrelated to the student's concerns, ideas, goals, and learning style, the teacher may produce only incompetence and a feeling of inadequacy in that student. If the teacher wants to help the student to become competent and to develop a view of himself as an adequate person, he has no choice but to start where the student is, to go where the student wants to and can go, and to help the student to get where he is going in the manner he wants to go.

The implication of meeting students where they are is that it is the teacher and not the student who must be ready. More specifically, we know that each student brings to school a unique set of experiences that have occurred primarily within the context of his family. His family has its own set of values, its own set of beliefs about what are the important things in life, and its own way of trying to solve problems. The student brings these particular experiences, values, and ways of dealing with his environment to the school with some expectation that classroom life will help him make some sense out of his experiences and help him to go beyond them and in the direction he wants his life to take. However, if a teacher establishes a particular set of values and organizes many sets of specific information and skills that he wants the student to acquire, and if he has certain expectations about what the student should be able to do when he enters the school, while he is there, and when he leaves, then more often than not what the student brings to school is going to collide with the teacher's predetermined classroom curriculum and methods and with his expectations of the student. Most likely the student will find little connection between life outside the classroom and what the teacher provides and expects of him. In the past, a responsibility was always placed on the student to adapt to the school's expectation of him. We now recognize that the burden of responsibility in providing a service must rest with the practitioner and not with the client (142). Consequently, the real question is, "Is the teacher ready to teach the student where the student is?" Teachers cannot, on the one hand, arbitrarily expect each student to learn and achieve according to their predetermined standards or according to standards irrelevant to students' skills and learning styles, and, on the other hand, feel justified in "explaining" a student's failure to meet their expectations or standards by claiming that the student has a "learning deficiency," e.g., "insufficient intelligence," or "low motivation," or "inadequate language development." When a teacher claims that students "fail" because they have learning deficiencies, he is ignoring or rejecting where the students are and what they bring to school. He is succumbing to a series of myths, beginning with the myth that there is the "average" student, which is followed by a second myth, that those students who differ from the average student are the "special" students, e.g., "slow learners" and "problem students." These two myths inevitably give rise to other myths, such as "the student is not ready," or "the student is not motivated." Carried to its logical conclusion, the most destructive of all myths emerges, namely, that when a student does not achieve grade level or when he does not learn at the expected rate or when he makes too many errors, he is a *failure*.

It is incomprehensible how a student who works to the best of his ability, expends his best efforts consistently, but does not come up to the average for his age and grade, can be viewed as a failure. Failing a student because he did not achieve grade level is as absurd as telling a child on his seventh birthday that he cannot be seven because he has not grown as tall or as heavy as the "average" seven-year-old in the neighborhood. No one would think of punishing the child to make him grow taller or heavier. No one would think of making a child "repeat" his seventh year of life or of telling the child that he is unacceptable as he is or of preventing him to live out his eighth year. Yet schools constantly require students to "repeat" a grade in which they have already done as well as their skills and available learning conditions permit, and publicly label them "failures" and declare them unacceptable for the next grade because they have not learned as much as the "average" student did in that grade (17).

The teacher who takes the position that the student who does not achieve at or above grade level or who does not meet his expectations is lacking in some human quality, is denying that each student is a unique individual, is violating the student's integrity as a person, and is running the risk of sowing the seeds of hate and bitter retribution in the hearts of the students who are failed. The teacher must accept the fact that there is no "average" student; there are only unique individuals, each with his own concerns, skills, and learning style; and the teacher's responsibility is to identify these individual differences and arrange learning conditions accordingly.

A doctor does not require his patients to ready their bodies for a group treatment that might be totally unrelated to their individual needs, e.g., a pint of blood, or cobalt treatment, or an injection of insulin. On the contrary, the doctor first makes an individual diagnosis and then prescribes an individual treatment. So the teacher must individualize his program for each student.

Further, in order to treat effectively the patient's particular physical condition, the doctor continually secures detailed information about the patient's response to treatment. He checks the patient's physical signs to determine whether the present form of treatment is working. He also needs to know from the patient what his perceptions are about the treatment. Consequently he asks, "How do you feel today?" or "How are you finding the medication?" On the basis of feedback from both the patient's physical signs and his perceptions of the treatment, the doctor makes some judgments about the effectiveness of his present methods and whether a new method of treatment is needed. He determines, for example, whether or not medication should be eliminated, supplemented, or altered in dosage, or whether a totally different form of medical intervention is needed. In any case, it is the doctor who must adapt to the patient's behavior.

Likewise it is the teacher who must be ready to meet the needs of the student. The teacher must accurately diagnose the individual student's knowledge, skills, and concerns both when the student enters the classroom and when the teacher is ready to plan a new learning program. The teacher must then plan and organize a learning program with the student that is consonant with the diagnosis—with what the student can and wants to do. The teacher then must continually gather reliable information about how effective his teaching methods are, how well his students are learning, and whether or not some changes are needed in his teaching methods.

Since the concept of meeting students where they are can be easily misunderstood, it may be helpful to clarify what it means and does not mean for the teacher.

Meeting students where they are means that, after the teacher determines where they are, he makes available to each student various kinds of activities, experiences, and instruction in areas and at levels that help the student go as far as he can and wants to go in developing his potentialities. After the teacher starts where they are, he exposes other forms of reality to the students, and with the new forms of reality he helps them clarify and evaluate their feelings and ideas; he helps them to design alternative pathways by which they can explore, experiment with ideas and materials, and confront personal and social conflicts; and he encourages them to seek their own answers and solutions to the questions and issues they find important.

Meeting the student where he is does not mean that some students will be "getting by" with less effort and contribution than others. If we believe that all students should be doing the same amount of work on a task, some students would indeed be getting by, since some students can discover faster and more easily than others. But when activities are adapted to the student's skills and rate of learning, the teacher is helping each student identify and commit himself to the types and levels of activities that help him do his best learning. For example, in order to do their best learning, some students may choose to discover more about a social problem by seeing it reenacted in a movie or a filmstrip; other students may discover best by reading about the problem in a book. Some may prefer to gather data and write a story about the problem; others may elect to act out the problem in a dramatization. Still other students may want to discuss or debate the problem.

Meeting students where they are also requires the teacher to provide differing amounts of guidance for different students. This means that the rule "treat each child the same" does not apply in some aspects of classroom life. Many teachers get "hung up" on the meaning of the word *fairness*. They believe that students will perceive them as "playing favorites" if they provide more guidance for some students than others or demand more of some students than others. However, students generally do not become envious or angry over such inconsistency if the teacher lets them know that he is treating students differently only because they have different needs; that from day to day even the same student will require different kinds and amounts of guidance because of his current concerns and skills, the task, the state of his health, and his mood; and that unless each student receives the help that is appropriate for him he cannot succeed in his learning efforts. However, the teacher makes it clear that treating each student differently does not mean that he cares less about the rights and welfare of some students, or that some students are not required to make a commitment to complete a learning program, or that some students are permitted to break a commitment after a program has been selected. Nor does it mean that the teacher will not hold each student to the rules for facilitating constructive interpersonal and group behavior.

In summary, in order to help each student be successful in his search for meaning and competence and become a productive and resourceful member of society, the teacher must be ready to help the student discover who he is, where he is, where he wants to and can go, and how he can best get there. The teacher must start with the student's ideas, skills, concerns, and goals. He must interact with each student as an individual and on his own terms. He must discover the student's current capabilities and concerns each day and arrange the conditions that help the student acquire the skills he needs to become a competent problem-solver and to develop a feeling of self-worth.

5

Building Freedom and Commitment in a Shared Environment

THE ULTIMATE PURPOSE of meeting students where they are is to help them acquire the skills to set their own goals, to plan their own learning activities, to rely on their own resourcefulness to be successful, and to evaluate for themselves the effectiveness and relevance of their efforts and behavior. If the teacher prizes a student for himself, he not only needs to adapt his behavior and classroom events to the student's current skills, concerns, and style of learning, but he also needs to help the student learn to direct his own learning.

Unfortunately, too many teachers make it impossible for a student to assume more and more responsibility for his own education. Far from helping him to develop into a resourceful, self-disciplined individual, they seem to do everything they can to keep him in a state of chronic dependency. Whatever rhetoric these teachers may subscribe to, education is, in practice, for them something they do to a student, and not something the student does to himself with the teacher's help. Even the concept of "individualized instruction" is for many teachers made to fit in the context of manipulation and control: a student is free to learn at his own rate that which the teacher permits him to learn. It is interesting to note that Plato defines a slave as "the person who executes the wishes of another." When a teacher makes all the decisions and a student is only a helpless recipient of the teacher's orders, intellectual and psychological slavery is the consequence.

It is a basic distrust of students' motives and a belief that they are not capable of managing their own learning that compel the teacher to use his behavior to control students. The teacher's control and use of power are perhaps most clearly revealed in the evaluation process. The teacher's appraisals have a profound influence on the present and future of each student, and the teacher continually makes compelling and often irrevocable judgments about the student's behavior. The student comes to know in clear terms when things are "right" or "wrong," "good" or "bad," "straight" or "crooked," "neat" or "messy," "beautiful" or "ugly." No one who has observed a classroom for any length of time has failed to be impressed by the frequency and absoluteness with which the teacher performs this function (92).

Teacher control is revealed in other ways, too. Students are denied the opportunity to talk about their lives, to plan their learning, to make educational decisions, to make significant contributions to the school, and to be important to or feel needed by teachers. Each day they learn that the school does not belong to them, that it is controlled and directed by others, and that rules are established and enforced by others. In short, they learn that they have little power to control any aspect of their school life.

It is interesting to note that while teachers insist on their right to have equal voice in all decisions that directly affect their behavior and welfare, they deny students the right to have equal voice in all decisions that directly affect *their* behavior and welfare.

When teachers take the position that the young cannot be trusted to direct their own learning, a teacher–student dichotomy is created. "After all," the teachers say, "we are teachers because we know, and students are students because they don't know." The teacher–student dichotomy, of course, places the student in a hopeless dilemma. On the one hand, he has a need to explore, to find meaning, and to become competent in his own way. He has his own rhythm for learning and developing. On the other hand, the standards of acceptable learning and the learning opportunities themselves are established by others. Other people have predetermined for the student what is an acceptable rate of learning and what is an acceptable goal to achieve. In such a dilemma the student often chooses one of two alternatives: he may adapt his behavior where possible to the teacher-established goals and processes and thereby become in the eyes of the teacher a "good" student; or he may resist the teacher's demands, assert his individuality, and thereby become for both the teacher and the administration a "troublemaker." Regardless of whether the student chooses one of these alternatives or yet another one, he does not discover and develop the best that is in him. He expends his available energy to devise and employ a variety of behavior strategies for dealing with his internal conflict, rather than for releasing his potential in personally satisfying and productive ways.

Teachers must recognize that to be distrusted is to be placed in a terribly disquieting and degrading position. No one likes to feel that he is not trustworthy, that he cannot exercise any control over his destiny. Each student wants to be respected as an equal. He wants to be given more power to shape the decisions which have a bearing on his own life.

He wants teachers to stop trying to take up each minute of his life both inside and outside the classroom by continually predesigning all classroom activities and arbitrarily assigning readings, book reports, term papers, and homework. He wants to live out his childhood and adolescence according to his sense of himself. He wants the chance to discover who he is and what he wants to do with his life.

He wants teachers who accept and value the reality he sees and knows outside the classroom. He wants classrooms in which he can continually report his personal observations, express his ideas, engage in discussion and debate, and interpret and evaluate the meaning of his life. He wants classroom experiences that help him to develop the understanding and skills he needs to deal adequately with the entire range of problems that confronts him *now*.

He wants teachers to stop demanding that he "work up to his ability," since no one ever does this anyway, including teachers. If he doesn't work up to his ability, he feels that it is a matter that he will decide for himself. He wants to be accepted for what he wants to learn and the rate at which he wants to learn. He wants to set his own goals, make his own contributions, and establish his own performance standards. He wants to be given more freedom to choose—even to make poor choices—and he wants to learn to live with the consequences of his choices.

When we consider each person's rights under law as interpreted by the Supreme Court in 1967 (*In re* Gault)—i.e., that "neither the Fourteenth Amendment nor the Bill of Rights is for adults alone"—and when we consider the evidence that all students, even "troublemakers," can respond constructively in an atmosphere in which they are valued and trusted, we must conclude that the "teacher-student relationship" must be redefined.

The same conclusion must also be reached when we consider that educational goals and means are interwoven and inseparable. One must be coordinated with the other. If our goals stress the development of individuals who are self-directed, self-disciplined, self-responsible, and capable of making intelligent choices, then our means must not be such that control and responsibility are taken away. A youngster cannot achieve the goal of becoming a self-directed learner if all the freedom and power to make decisions related to his learning are held by others.

Consequently, the teacher and student must be partners in education. They must have equal voice in making real choices in all matters that concern them. In the classroom this means an equal voice in selecting (*1*) the goals—the knowledge and skills to be acquired; (*2*) the means—the planning and implementation of learning activities, the methods, materials, and aids for learning; and (*3*) the progress appraisals—the judgments about what has been learned, what has not been learned, what needs to be pursued, and how it needs to be pursued. Equal voice in the classroom also applies to establishing and enforcing rules of conduct, evaluating and revising the curriculum, and assessing the quality of teaching.

It is a shared world and a shared society, and it should therefore be a shared classroom with rights and responsibilities applying equally to both the student and the teacher. The teacher and student must view education as an ongoing interaction of making responsible demands on each other and protecting each other's rights with agreements and decisions arrived at in the absence of compulsion on the part of either person. In a shared classroom the teacher does not dominate students. The student directs his own behavior. However, self-direction is not synonomous with *absolute* freedom. Absolute freedom is a myth when two or more people have to share the same environment. Freedom always exists in a social context. Nor does self-direction mean "doing one's own thing." This brand of indifferent self-reliance, of insensitivity in interpersonal relations, is also a form of insanity that is responsible for increasing alienation and social suffering. Self-direction must always be viewed as occurring in an environment of *shared* needs, rights, and responsibilities. Therefore, self-direction in a shared classroom by definition requires a student to be both free and socially responsible.

Since the schools are to provide a forum for developing skilled and socially responsible individuals, teachers have the right to require much of their students and are in fact irresponsible when they do not make demands on them. However, these requirements are not that all students must read specific pages or chapters in a given book, or work on specific problems or tasks; the specifics to be completed are always in terms of the individual student's level of awareness, skills, and concerns in the subject. What each teacher has the right to demand and expect is that the student, with the teacher's help, select a learning program comprised of goals and activities that lead the student to acquire new skills or improve his present skills in the subject, and commit himself to completing the selected learning program. Freedom in the context of a shared society also obligates the teacher to require *group* learning programs, with each student selecting and commiting himself to achieve group goals, employ group procedures, and develop group skills for solving problems and answering questions. If students are to recognize that cooperation is more than a platitude, that it is a necessary condition of justice and order in a society, then group-selected, -implemented, and -evaluated learning programs must be required. Students need to learn that the group activity is designed not for its own sake but to help them learn that people are interdependent, that people need one another to succeed and to survive, and that some ways of behaving strengthen a society while others destroy it.

The student is also entitled to require much from his teacher. He has the right to demand and expect that the teacher respect him as a unique person; that the learning goals, activities, and materials be relevant and tailored to his concerns and his skills; and that the teacher provide him with the kind of guidance he needs, when he needs it. If the student has difficulty selecting a learning program, the teacher has a responsibility to suggest a large range of relevant alternatives. The student in turn has a responsibility to make a choice and to commit himself to that choice. Moreover, since it is from commitment that a student will gain maturity in self-responsibility and self-discipline, he may not be excused from fulfilling a commitment. If a teacher accepts an excuse, the student will most likely learn that commitments and promises need not be kept, and that one does not have to persist to achieve worthwhile goals. If it is discovered that a learning program is inappropriate, alternative programs need to be identified, and the student needs to commit and recommit himself for as long as it takes to complete a program based on his skills and concerns and within the context of the shared classroom.

In failing to keep a commitment and to persist at completing a selected learning program, the student does not give himself the chance he needs to discover that he can succeed, that he already has some useful skills, and that he is a worthy person. This is especially true for the student with a negative picture of himself. When he does not carry out a commitment, he merely reaffirms the picture he has of himself as an incompetent, weak, dependent, frightened, and lonely person. However, when the teacher requires and helps the student to plan worthwhile learning goals and activities, and when the teacher accepts no excuse from him for not fulfilling his commitments, the student begins to see himself as capable of meeting the challenges he finds in his world (58).

The teacher must continually bear in mind that freedom and commitment always go together in the classroom. He must avoid the error that some "open classroom" teachers slip into at the primary level, namely, the belief that if a student is simply provided with the freedom to learn, he will *necessarily* develop useful skills. Freedom to learn in the absence of a commitment to pursue a particular goal for a specified period of time often encourages the student only to drift from activity to activity without any sense of direction or continuity. It is when the teacher requires a specific commitment from the student that he helps him to explore fully his interests and abilities and to focus his attention and energies long enough on tasks to acquire useful skills.

The teacher may be prompted to ask at this point, "If it is true that a student's interests change and that it is undesirable to require him to complete an activity if his interest is gone, how can we insist that the student make a commitment and that he not be excused from the commitment?" The reply is that a commitment must be limited to a reasonable period of time, and that a reasonable period of time for each student is discovered by observing the student's behavior. If a student tends to stay with a task for a very short time, the teacher must find out why the student has lost interest in it and failed to complete it. The teacher must look for ways to lengthen the student's interest span, e.g., provide the student with more stimulating materials or more detailed information about the effectiveness of his learning strategies. As his interest span slowly lengthens, the teacher must pace the length of commitments accordingly.

A second question may be raised: "Aren't many students unable to use freedom constructively because of authoritarian parents and previous teachers who were dictatorial?" To be sure, freedom can be threatening to some students at first. Also, there are some students who, when given a great deal of freedom, lose sight of the social context of learning and therefore tend to misuse it. It is also true that most students are so used to responding to the needs and concerns of teachers that it may take a long time for them to discover the things that concern them most. Undoubtedly, providing the conditions for helping each student develop freedom in a shared context will be very trying for the teacher. He will become frustrated and bewildered when he and his students are groping for the appropriate amounts of structure, when some of his students are afraid to make commitments, and when some of them test his determination to enforce each of the commitments they make.

However, movement toward a shared classroom need not be a traumatic experience if the teacher recognizes that he should make changes at a rate that is also comfortable for *him*. Consequently, it may be advantageous to both the teacher and student if at first the teacher has a greater voice than the student in planning some, although not all, of the components of his learning program. For example, the teacher may need to have a larger role than the student in either selecting the goals to be achieved, planning the types of activities to be completed, formulating the general rules of conduct to be followed, or establishing the program schedule, performance deadlines, and grading consequences to be implemented. The teacher may also find that a written agreement or contract is most effective in getting a student started. Gradually the teacher can help the student assume an equal voice in managing all aspects of his learning. (Examples of how the teacher can employ a written contract and help his students direct their own learning will be found in Chapters 7, 8, and 10.)

What results can be expected from freeing students to learn and helping them use their freedom constructively in a shared classroom? There is evidence that indicates each of the following (34, 68, 145): (*1*) When students feel that they have a voice and have influence, they are likely to believe that others view them as competent and trustworthy individuals. (*2*) When students feel that they are competent and trusted individuals, they are likely to act responsibly when they are asked to make commitments and when they are left unsupervised. (*3*) When students work jointly with others in making decisions that affect their lives, they view themselves and their environment more realistically and can accept disappointment and frustration without being destructive.

Let me try to summarize the basic points I have tried to communicate about the behavior of the teacher. Many teachers assume that since our way of life requires laws, they will have a law-abiding student when they have a controlled one. As a consequence, they teach the importance of conformity and obedience to authority. They operate their classrooms in a climate of threat and distrust. The teacher *knows,* and that is why he is the teacher; the student *does not know,* and that is why he is the student. He who doesn't know is required to listen; he who knows has been endowed to tell. "Readiness" and "motivation" on the part of the listening learner are assumed. Proof of learning is supplied by test-taking procedures that, like the goals and activities, are predesigned by the teacher. Virtually all teaching decisions are designed to encourage each student to conform to the teacher's concept of "good" behavior and "good" achievement levels.

However, since the basic responsibility of the teacher is to help each student become a competent learner and view himself as having worth in his own right, the teacher is obligated to provide the student with the trust and support he needs to direct and evaluate his own learning. The nature of learning suggests unmistakably that people do their best learning when they are prized as individuals in their own right and when they are given the help they need to search and discover in their own way. Consequently, the teacher must start by accepting the student's raison d'être and by accepting the student's concerns, skills, and goals as the basis for making teaching decisions. The teacher will have to accept the student's language, dress, and values as the starting point— not as a psychological device to lure him eventually into accepting the teacher's predetermined notions of "the true," "the good," and "the beautiful," but as the only way to help the student to explore the meaning of his own life, to achieve competency in personal and social skills, and to feel adequate and worthy as a person.

The extent to which the teacher accepts, trusts, and meets the student where he is, will be reflected by the extent to which the dichotomy between "teaching" and "learning" is dissolved; the extent to which the teacher and student are partners in a shared environment; the extent to which the teacher and student develop their humanity and potentialities together.

If teachers are to help students learn in personally and socially advantageous ways, they must behave as equals with students, they must create shared classrooms. They can create shared classrooms by prizing and trusting students and requiring commitments, rather than by relying on coercion and force. Competency, a feeling of self-worth, and democracy can be effectively learned in our schools if our teaching techniques are modified—if we replace the teacher-owned classroom with the shared classroom.

III

THE SHARED CLASSROOM

6

Finding Out Where the Student Is

IN ORDER FOR the teacher to discover each student's current concerns, competencies, and style of learning, he needs to ask: What are the student's interests and activities outside of school? What skills does he bring to school? What does he already know about my subject? What can he teach me about how he learns? What does he talk about when adults are not watching him or telling him how to talk and what to say? How does he see himself as a person? How does he view the people and events in his life and the things he reads and hears about, e.g., fighting, drugs, death, policemen, hospitals, love, parents, religion, peers, money, power, war? What is his way of exploring and interacting in a situation? How does he test an idea? Is he persistent or does he become easily discouraged? Does he need support from others? Does he prefer to read about, talk about, listen to, or act out something to grasp its meaning? What people in his life and what parts of his day are most important to him? What attitudes does he have toward learning in general, toward teachers, toward this subject, and toward classroom participation? Does he have any personal problems that may interfere with classroom learning? What are his expectations of the school and what does he expect of me?

These are some of the questions to which the teacher needs to find answers, and they imply that he will have to suspend his beliefs about how his students should perform. They imply that he will not decide how and what he will teach his students *before* they enter the classroom; that he will rely not on IQ scores or grade-level achievement tests but on the students themselves to find out where they are; that he will not waste the student's time and his own time in "teaching" the student what he already knows or what he doesn't need or want to know; that he will take each student as he finds him and will discover what he can and wants to do and give him a fresh opportunity to learn and to become the kind of person he wants to be.

There are many ways to find out where each student is; some of the most useful are: (*1*) observing the kinds of behavior the student displays in informal activities with others, (*2*) devising classroom events and techniques that enable the student to project his feelings about the people and events in his life, and (*3*) designing and administering diagnostic tests that allow the student to disclose some of the knowledge and skills he has already acquired in the subject.

Observing Behavior during Informal Activities

The teacher can perhaps best discover the kinds of learning activities a student wants to and can complete by carefully observing his behavior in unstructured situations. More specifically, an enormous amount of useful information can be quickly gathered by taking the time to talk to each student about his dreams, his hopes, and his problems and by taking the time to listen to his language style, his ideas, his feelings, his preferences, and his view about himself as he talks with his peers before class, in the cafeteria, and in hallways.

The student's language especially reflects his way of thinking, feeling, and responding to his experiences and to his present situation. For example, much about the way a student feels about himself, his parents, his peers, or anything else can be discovered from observing the intonations and tempo he uses when he talks— from whether or not he hesitates, is quick, "square," deliberate, loud, soft, "cool," angry, and so on. It will be recalled that Herbert Kohl carefully observed the language of his thirty-six children, especially Ralph's exchanges with Michael, to discover more about their ideas, feelings, and skills and to try to help them learn more about themselves and their environment (88).

When the teacher arranges leisure or play activities for students, he can also find out much about their ideas, feelings, and ways of learning. Unfortunately, too many teachers view students' play as silly stuff or goofing off. However, play is important business for young people, because they are trying to find answers to what are, for them, very serious questions—questions about their fears, their strengths, and their courage; questions about the ways in which they can make things happen; and questions about the ways in which they are acceptable to others. If a teacher wants to understand how best to help his students learn, he must discover more about the meanings they find in play and leisure activities and he must design more informal, open-ended situations that enable them to communicate the ideas, feelings, and concerns that are important to them.

Much about a student can be discovered when he is encouraged to bring to class and talk about the things he cares about and uses outside the class. He can also demonstrate in class a skill he has acquired outside the school, whether it be in art, athletics, crafts, or mechanics. "Teach Me" and "Tell Me" sessions are two ways of having students select a skill or hobby they would like to show others or select a topic or problem they would like to discuss with others, and in the process disclose how they think and feel and what they value and enjoy.

If the teacher would like to employ this technique the first day of class, he can begin with introductions and then take the students on a twenty-minute "tour of the subject" to show them what is available—the materials, the activities, and the resources. During the tour he can suggest some of the activities they might like to try. After the tour he can let each student, on his own or in pairs or small groups, explore and discuss his concerns and preferences. After a short period of time, the teacher can ask students if they have found anything interesting that they would like to pursue or if they would like to select or plan something and whether he can help them in some way. The teacher can then set up a "Teach Me" or "Tell Me" session in which each student can take anything he wishes from the classroom or from outside to describe or demonstrate to the class, or he can make up a question or problem that he would like to discuss.

Each student's level of awareness, interests, and style of learning need to be discovered, not to seduce the student into eventually doing what the teacher wants done, but so the teacher can become an adult in the student's life who can help him find himself and become the kind of person he wants to become. Consequently, experiences, feelings, ideas, fears, and hopes need to be exchanged. Each member of the class must try to discover more about himself, about each of the other class members, and about the subject in order to learn how the class, the subject, and the activities can be shared experiences and how each class member can help the others make relevant decisions about learning.

Other activities can be designed to encourage each student to share something about himself with the classroom group. One such activity is to arrange chairs in a circle so that the teacher and students can see one another, and then have each group member, starting with the teacher, go to the blackboard, write his name clearly, and tell something about himself to the group. The choice of information to be revealed would be left up to each group member but might include such things as hobbies, after-school activities, heroes, favorite TV programs, dislikes, and so forth. After returning to his seat, each member would make a placecard for himself from a page of notebook paper folded in half. He would print his name on the bottom half of the card and place the card over the edge of his desk or table so that everyone could see his name. Some students might prefer to wear name tags for a few days. (At the elementary level the learning of names could also be turned into a spelling activity, with each student making his own spelling list of all class members and then spelling and pronouncing each name.)

Another classroom procedure is to devise a panel interview called "Who Am I?" The teacher would select at random four or five students who comprise a panel of interviewers to ask each student questions as though each student were a visiting "celebrity" whose identity was not known. The questions would be designed to elicit information that the panel thinks all members of the group would like to know. The "celebrity" could choose not to answer any questions that make him uncomfortable. The process would continue until all group members have been interviewed, with the teacher appointing a new panel of interviewers from time to time.

Still another procedure that can be used to learn about each student, especially to discover how he responds when a group is asked to organize itself and cooperate, is to devise a situation that requires the total classroom group to find an answer to a particular question or to solve a particular problem or to pursue a specific goal. So that he may learn about students' *natural* ways of responding, the teacher should not provide any guidelines or suggestions on how to organize the group or how to gather and share information. The natural behavior of each student in a group activity can help the teacher discover the different ways in which students interact with each other, the different roles they assume, and the amount of guidance each needs in order to complete an activity successfully.

Group puzzle problems also are excellent opportunities for finding out more about students' learning styles. For example, the teacher could give the following directions to a group of upper elementary or high school students seated in a circle (153):

> Today you are going to solve a murder mystery. I have in my hand several slips of paper, and on each slip is written one clue. Each clue is necessary to solve the murder mystery. When all the clues are examined together you will be able to determine five things: (*1*) the victim, (*2*) the weapon that was used, (*3*) the time of the murder, (*4*) the place of the murder, and (*5*) the murderer. I will pass out a clue to each of you, but because of the size of our class some of you may need to share your clue or be given more than one clue. The rules for solving the mystery are the following. You must organize yourselves to find out *each* of the five pieces of information about the murder, namely, the

victim, the *murderer,* the *method,* the *time,* and the *place.* I will
need to have *all five answers.* If you give me an incorrect answer
I will simply inform you that the answer is incorrect and that you
must continue your search. I will not give any hints or suggestions.
This is *your* mystery to solve. Also, all communications among
yourselves must be *verbal.* You may not pass around, share, or
collect the written clues. You must remain in your seats and solve
the mystery by *talking and exchanging ideas.* Here are the clues.
[The clues for the puzzle problem are to be found in Appendix A.]

The directions would be repeated until all the students
understand them. Then the teacher would step away and not talk
to the group until the mystery is solved. He would observe how
each student responds to the situation, e.g., whether he is quick
to assume leadership, whether he is detached from the group,
whether he is dependent or "lost," whether he is impulsive or
reflective, whether he remains cool or becomes emotional; how he
collaborates with others; and how he communicates, i.e., his tempo,
his phraseology, his colloquialisms, and his gestures.

When the group has completed the activity, the teacher would
have each student talk about how he perceived the situation. The
student might be asked, "Did you feel at first that you might be
unable to find all five answers?" "Did you enjoy working as a
group to solve the murder mystery or would you have preferred
to do something by yourself?" "If you had been appointed the
leader of this group, how would you have felt?" "Was the puzzle
problem frustrating to you?"

Many kinds of similar useful activities can be devised by the
teacher to learn about students. Many problem- and riddle-type
puzzles appropriate for the classroom may also be found in popular monthly publications such as *Reader's Digest.* The pamphlet
Learning Discussion Skills Through Games (153) also describes
a number of puzzle problems and techniques for encouraging
students to demonstrate how they go about trying to solve their
problems.

Informal Projective Techniques

If the teacher finds that his observations of informal class interactions do not provide him with the information needed to help each student design an appropriate learning program, he can gather additional valuable information by designing procedures that encourage the student to report how he views himself; how he feels about his school, his peers, his teachers; and what he prefers most to learn about and what he prefers least. One such procedure is to give the student a sentence-completion form. The teacher may have to design his own, since commercially available ones often do not ask the kinds of questions that provide the teacher with relevant information. One classroom-tested form that the teacher may find applicable to his students is "How I Feel" (fig. 1). If students cannot read well, the teacher could arrange seats in a circle, read aloud each incomplete sentence, and ask the students to complete each sentence orally. The teacher can jot down each youngster's responses or record them on tape. A more useful form for students who read well but do not write very clearly would be a checklist such as "How I See Myself" (fig. 2).

The teacher may also find it effective to show a film in which a variety of problems and topics in a subject are explored or in which students of the same age level as his class are engaged in activities relevant to the subject under consideration. A discussion following the film could be held to give each student the opportunity to report to the teacher and the class some of the problems, issues, and questions in the subject which are of particular concern to him.

Some teachers may find that they can learn a great deal about how students see themselves when each student makes a face mask and describes it to the class. Using $8\frac{1}{2} \times 11$ unlined paper, the student can cut out a face with scissors or tear one out with his fingers and then draw or color in different features and designs in any way he wishes with crayons, pencils, or other materials. He would be free to include or omit anything he chose, making the mask either the way he sees himself or the way he believes

Date_____
Your name_____
Subject_____
Teacher_____

How I Feel

Below are thirty unfinished sentences that you are to complete.
You are to finish them any way you wish. This is not a test. There
are no right or wrong answers. What is true for you would not
necessarily be true for somebody else. For example, one student
finished the incomplete sentence "Homework is ..." with the words
"helpful when you need to practice something." What is most true
for him about homework is that it is helpful when practice is needed.
You must complete each sentence according to what you feel is most
true about you. Again, there are no correct or incorrect answers.
The way you feel about things is what counts.

1. The things I like to learn about most are ....
2. After school I ....
3. I like a teacher who is ....
4. When a teacher asks me questions I ....
5. In the evening I like to ....
6. I get mad when ....
7. The best thing about school is ....
8. Someday I ....
9. I wish teachers would ....
10. I like to read about ....
11. When answering questions aloud in class I ....
12. I can't learn when ....
13. What I like to do most is ....
14. I hate ....
15. When I am by myself I ....
16. If I were a teacher I would ....
17. The worst thing about school is ....
18. When I go on a field trip I ....
19. My parents ....
20. The programs I like to watch most on TV are ....
21. I often wish ....
22. When I go to the library I ....
23. I am happiest when ....
24. Homework is ....
25. I learn best when ....
26. When I work with other students, I ....
27. When I learn by myself, I ....
28. If I failed in school I would ....
29. When a teacher asks me to find the answers
     to my own questions I ....
30. If teachers could be different they should ....

Figure 1.

How I See Myself

Place a check (✓) mark in front of the statement that is true for you.

1. I get mad easily and explode.
2. I stay with something until I finish it.
3. I'm not very good in a lot of things.
4. I like to work with others.
5. I don't like to work on committees.
6. I wish I were a different height.
7. I worry a lot.
8. I wish I could do something with my hair.
9. Teachers don't like me.
10. I haven't much energy.
11. I don't play games very well.
12. I'm just the right weight.
13. I'm good at speaking before a group.
14. I wish I were better-looking.
15. I get along well with teachers.
16. I don't like teachers.
17. I like to try new things.
18. I can do good work in school.
19. I get sick a lot.
20. I don't like to work alone.
21. I know how to plan my time.
22. I'm very good at making things with my hands.
23. School is very interesting.
24. I'm happy with the way I am.
25. I'm not as smart as the others.
26. My clothes are not very nice.
27. I don't read well.
28. I learn new things easily.
29. I'm always getting into trouble.
30. I like it better when I can work with a classmate instead of the teacher.

Figure 2.

others see him. When all the students have completed their masks, they can sit in a circle formation and, going around the circle, each student can describe his mask to the others. The teacher will find it very helpful to establish the rule that no student may laugh at or criticize any mask except his own. Such a rule often helps to minimize the possibility that some students will mock other students' masks and spoil what could otherwise be a valuable experience for the entire class.

Diagnostic Tests

In addition to informal projective techniques, the teacher may also design and administer a diagnostic test to discover some of the student's current knowledge and skills in a particular subject. This may be quite informal, with the teacher saying to the class, "I have some questions (or words or numbers or problems or pictures) that I would like to share with you and would like to know what you think about them or might want to do." Informal diagnostic tests allow the teacher to observe interaction between students. At the elementary level, children could be divided into small groups to examine words, pictures, or objects for a fifteen- or twenty-minute period, with the teacher moving from group to group to observe students' language, interpersonal skills, and concerns. More specifically, an elementary teacher trying to find out where his students are in vocabulary may say to them: "I have some words here on a card that might make us think of the things we would most like to do or talk about. Let's see what these words mean to each of us." The elementary teacher can do the same thing with numbers for math, pictures for social studies, and so on. Also, ditto sheets presenting questions and problems at various difficulty levels in a subject can be distributed to each student. The sheets can require each student to complete some activities by himself and other activities with groups of different sizes.

Some teachers may find it necessary to devise a comprehensive pencil-and-paper diagnostic test to identify specific student skills or to obtain specific information about a student's knowledge in a given subject (91). In such a situation a teacher may find the following set of procedures helpful:

STEP 1: List a *set of objectives* that you believe are desirable to achieve in the subject.

STEP 2: Identify *areas of competency* that students would have to master to achieve the objectives.

STEP 3: Take each competency area individually and write out *performance questions*—questions that ask the student to display each of the specific concepts or skills that comprise the competency area. The task is easier if you first write out the questions that ask the student to demonstrate the most complex concepts or skills in the competency area and then ask yourself, "In order for the student to demonstrate these, what are the immediate prerequisite concepts and skills that he needs to acquire?" Then write out the questions, testing for the presence of these lower-level concepts and skills, until performance questions tapping all of the concepts and skills that comprise the competency area have been identified. Follow this procedure for each competency area.

STEP 4: Place all of the performance questions for each competency area together and administer them to the student to determine which concepts and skills he has acquired in each competency area and those he has not acquired.

Let me illustrate a partial use of these steps for a field of study labeled *Human Nutrition*. The objectives in *Human Nutrition* are to have each student (*1*) explain why the body needs certain nutrients to function adequately, and (*2*) describe how these nutrients are utilized by the body. Let's assume that one of the competency areas that need to be mastered to achieve the objectives would be the capability of explaining and comparing the different phases of human digestion. A question that would tap some of the complex concepts and skills involved in mastering this competency area might be, "How does the digestion process in the stomach compare with the digestion process in the small intestine?" The teacher might then determine that in order for the student to answer this question, he would need to employ several specific lower-level concepts and skills. Hence, the teacher might write out the following three questions, which would test for the presence of the necessary lower-level concepts and skills.

1. "How is food digested in the small intestine?"
2. "What are the effects of hydrochloric acid and pepsin on proteins?"
3. "What are the effects of mixing saliva with carbohydrates?"

The teacher would then place these performance questions together with performance questions relating to other essential competency areas and administer them to the student to determine the student's current competencies.

If the diagnostic test is to provide the teacher with some useful information about planning learning activities, the final list of performance questions should (1) be representative of the entire range of competencies the teacher believes are needed to achieve the objectives, and (2) reflect the relative importance each of the competency areas has in the subject (e.g., no one area should be overemphasized or minimized if all competency areas are of equal importance).

When the teacher reviews the student's diagnostic test performance, he should bear in mind that the student's *score* is relatively unimportant. The teacher's attention should be directed to each of the competency areas to which the student was asked to respond, and he should note the specific concepts and skills the student has acquired, for these disclose to some degree where the student is and where he can go next.

The limitations of diagnostic tests are extremely important to note. Although curriculum organizers and writers construct "course structures" or "learning hierarchies" in order to help teachers design useful diagnostic tests, such structures and hierarchies are often artificial. The *teacher* may understand the particular arrangements of words curriculum organizers use to describe concepts, principles, and skills. However, words become meaningful to a *student* only when *he* attaches meaning to them, and his own needs, concerns, and learning style will dictate what the meanings will be. A student's understanding and skill in a particular area cannot be discovered from a diagnostic test alone; nor is it possible to devise a test that taps all the knowledge and skills a student has in a given subject. Also, there is always the question of how much better a student would have performed if the very language of the diagnostic test were clearer and simpler or if the learning hierarchy were organized in a different way.

The learning hierarchy, or body of knowledge, that a teacher or curriculum writer organizes in designing a diagnostic test represents but one way to structure some of the important meanings and skills in a particular subject. Consequently, performance on a diagnostic test—or, for that matter, on any formal test of achievement—provides at best an incomplete picture of a student's current knowledge and skills in a particular subject. The basic value of any test lies in its ability to supplement other procedures, such as observation, informal inquiry sessions, informal projective techniques, and personal conferences for determining the kinds of skills a student can employ and the kinds of goals he can and wants to pursue (92). In fact, compared to a diagnostic test, more useful information may be secured by simply asking students to write out or say in their own words what they know, like best, like least, and would like to know and do with regard to specific topics, problems, and skills in a subject.

Preparing an Individual Learning Folder

After gathering information about each student's concerns, skills, and goals, the teacher should devise a method of making the information accessible to both himself and the student. One procedure for handling this information would be to prepare an individual learning folder, which would be a concise and convenient file of the student's important learning characteristics as discovered from informal activities, questionnaires, and diagnostic tests. Both teacher and student would have a learning folder and a copy of each set of materials placed in it.

The learning folder can provide a valuable reference when working with each student to plan a program, to assess his progress, and to revise a learning program when it becomes necessary. For example, the teacher can provide valuable suggestions to the student with regard to (*1*) the kind, number, and level of activities, materials, or tasks he may wish to pursue; (*2*) the learning methods or procedures he may wish to employ; (*3*) whether he might like to work by himself or with specific students; and (*4*) the length of time he might want to set aside for each of the activities and the total learning program. The learning folder can help the student and teacher plan for greater relevance, success, and satisfaction.

An up-to-date learning folder can also be a guide for determining whether broader experiences and learning opportunities need to be selected by a student. If it appears that the student is using only one or two ways of learning, additional activities can be devised to induce him to experiment with other ways. For example, if a student seems to be spending most of his time reading and then reporting on what he has read, the teacher could ask the student to broaden his learning base by reading about how to make something with his hands and then showing others what he has learned from his reading by actually making it. As each student moves into new learning media and approaches, a description of these methods can be added to the folder.

The learning folder could also include a record of each learning program planned for the student. This would enable the teacher to refer back to each of the student's original goals and plans when assessing his rate of progress, and to determine the extent to which the different procedures he used to find out where students were provided him with reliable information about the student's current knowledge, skills, concerns, and style of learning. The learning folder can be used by the student throughout the entire school term to keep copies of learning programs, samples of progress, notes on class discussions and conferences with the teacher, and daily entries about how he feels about his work and the way the class is working.

If the teacher is to help his students plan personally meaningful learning activities and succeed in their endeavors, he must suspend all of his expectations about the knowledge and skills they should possess when they enter the classroom. He must go to the students themselves to discover what they can and want to do and to determine the direction classroom life will take. He must organize his classroom in ways that enable his students— individually, in pairs, and in groups—to engage in a variety of structured and unstructured activities and to disclose where they are in their ideas, feelings, learning styles, skills, and hopes.

7

Planning Reality-oriented Activities Together

ONE OF THE teacher's most important roles in conducting a shared classroom is to help students discover how different kinds of activities, materials, and tasks can be made relevant to their concerns and goals and can move them toward the acquisition of valuable meanings and competencies. The teacher's obligation of relevance is achieved in classroom life not only when he meets the student where he is but also when he opens up reality for the student and demonstrates the applicability of different ideas and skills to his life. Although a relevant curriculum is one that helps the student make some sense out of his perceptual world, the teacher must organize the learning environment in a way that enables the student to extend the boundaries of his perceptual world. In a sense, then, the *teacher* becomes the curriculum by the way in which he helps students to understand the meaning of their lives and to explore the different directions their lives can take.

One way the teacher and students can create their own relevant, reality-oriented curriculum is by designing and conducting simulations—by reenacting or re-creating real-world transactions, conflicts, and problems in the classroom—to help students investigate and discover more directly how and why real-world events happen. Let me describe some uses of simulations in different subjects.

In economics, simulated conditions can be designed to help students understand the basic principles of supply and demand and how the economy works. Students can assume the characters, goals, and responsibilities of wholesalers, retailers, and consumers. The consumers would all buy certain essential goods and would also choose freely among other items. The object of the wholesalers and retailers would be to sell as much as they could at the highest profit. At first, wholesalers and retailers would set prices on their goods in a random fashion. During the simulation, students would learn that whether or not prices are too high depends partly on how many people want to buy their goods and how badly. By the time the simulated slice of reality is over, students would understand the basic mechanism of supply and demand, although they might not know the label for it (39).

History can be made relevant by beginning with the students' current experiences and the happenings and issues they value, and then, through simulation, examining how each of these items was experienced or handled during an earlier period in history. A student in one of my educational psychology classes taught world history this way in a so-called "problem" school. He had students list their concerns—sexual freedom, law, dress, war, status, power, influencing people, reforming government—and then, through role playing, they simulated conflicts and problems in each of these areas of concern and for each of the historical periods studied. The students also cut out pictures and stories from newspapers and magazines on fashions, contests, sports, religions, health foods, methods of treating illnesses, and so on, and then through simulations examined conflicts and concerns as they may have developed at different periods. By using this approach, the student teacher made two discoveries when the term ended. First, his students had achieved approximately 90 per cent of the "course" objectives as stated in the syllabus on file in the principal's office, although they had "covered" only 20 per cent of the textbook and the content listed in the syllabus. Second, there had been virtually no discipline problems in the class, and the teacher had the lowest incidence of "cutting" of any teacher over the previous four-year period.

L. Cuban (28) points out that when classroom activities simulate the concreteness and real-life conflicts and feelings that people experience, attention is captured and personally meaningful learning takes place. As a high school teacher in Cleveland's black ghetto, Cuban was successful in simulating real-life conflicts to make United States history come alive. For example, one day when his class was studying the causes of the Civil War, he led students to explore the part that the slavery issue played (103).

"All right," Cuban says. "Now, I say I could have prevented the Civil War. With Lincoln's idea—what was that?"

A girl says, "Compensated emancipation."

"What does that mean?"

"Buy the slaves from the Southerners and set them free."

"Would it have worked? Would it have prevented the Civil War?"

The class groans, "No."

"Why not?"

A number of ideas are thrown forth—the Northerners didn't want to spend the money, you couldn't have a set price, the whole system was based on slaves. A girl says, "The Southerners wouldn't do it because it would make the Negroes equal to them."

"Let's get back to Beard," Cuban says. "Here. Less than ten per cent of the Southerners owned slaves, but they all fought for slavery. How could they persuade the ninety per cent to fight? You try it." He addressed two Negro girls and a Negro boy seated at his extreme left. "You're the slave owners. The rest of the class doesn't own slaves. You persuade them to fight for you."

One girl, giggling, tries, "Those Yankees, they want to come down and take everything away from you."

"Oh, no, they don't," Cuban says. "Just from you. I don't have anything they want."

"Our whole economy is based on slaves," says the boy.

"No, sir," says a boy in the non-slaveholding section, falling into the spirit of the situation. "My economy isn't. I got to do my own work."

The debate rages for a while, Cuban grinning over it, objecting

where the 90 per cent can't find a reply. "Come on, now," he says.
"Why will these four million fight for four years? If you can't
come up with this, class, the whole thing is completely unreal, just
something in a textbook."

Finally, in the heat of the argument, one of the Negro girls in
the slaveholding section comes up with, "Remember those slave
rebellions? Remember what happened on those plantations? The
Yankees will come down here and raise up those Negroes to be
your equals, and there'll be no controlling them." The class roars
with laughter at her, and she bends her head.

"Let's give it a name," Cuban says. He writes on the board,
"WHITE SUPREMACY." He says, "Any of you ever hear of
U. B. Phillips?"

One boy has read it, and says, "He thinks that's the whole
theme of Southern history."

The one white boy in the class, a West Virginia redneck, now
makes his contribution: "You can find reasons all you like," he
says. "I think they fought because they were told to fight."

Cuban says, "Maybe. Now, when we discuss Reconstruction
we'll find this same argument of White Supremacy used to justify
. . . what? . . . anybody know?"

And a Negro boy says, "Segregation." [Pp. 159–60]

Simulations can also be designed to make the learning of foreign languages more than a series of memorization exercises. For
example, another student in one of my educational psychology
classes designed a series of "Mission Impossible" episodes to
make French more interesting and enjoyable to learn and teach.
During two class periods the learning of French centered around
the following episode:

Your mission, should you choose to accept it, is to go to the
French town of Vichy and rescue Madame Bonbon, whose photograph you are looking at. She is being held against her will as a
barmaid in a cabaret by her evil brother, Monsieur Méchant. His
photograph is enclosed.

You will be dropped by parachute, at *exactly* 10 A.M., outside
of the small French town of Vichy. There you will rent a car and
drive to the Source de l'Hôpital, where you will buy a bottle of the
famous mineral spring water (good for asthma, gout, diabetes,

malaria, skin rash, and headaches). At *exactly* 11 A.M. you will take your bottle of water and go to a cabaret called *Le Privé de l'Alhambra*, at No. 1, rue Sornin, where you will see Madame Bonbon working as a barmaid, under the watchful eye of Monsieur Méchant. She will know you by the bottle of mineral spring water that you will be carrying. Order one drink from her, and when you leave, slip her the following note of instructions, which you will need to translate into *French:*

"This afternoon at the racetrack at *exactly* 3 P.M., go to the bathroom and escape through the window. I wil be waiting to save you."

Monsieur Méchant and Madame Bonbon go to the racetrack every Saturday afternoon, and there you must make your contact. You must be waiting outside the bathroom window at *exactly* 3 P.M., at which time you will take Madame Bonbon to your car and drive to Allier airport, where a private plane will be waiting to bring you back to the U.S. In the event that you or other members of your force are captured by the secret police, you will need to make your own arrangements for getting back to the U.S. The only help we can offer is that you can make contact with a Monsieur Le Grand, a powerful leader of the underground, through the prison guard Dubré.

The teacher then asked the students to help her determine the interactional events that would actually occur in the episode, the roles that the students would have to assume, and the dialogue each actor would need to know.

Through "Mission Impossible" simulations and other concrete, reality-oriented methods, the students were able to learn French quickly and enjoyably. Even the "slow learners" progressed rapidly.

Perhaps simulations have the greatest potential when they help students explore the nature of and solutions to interpersonal, ethnic, politicial, racial, and socio-economic problems. Virtually every problem that reflects some degree of conflict between man and man can be dramatized fruitfully in the classroom. Since these problems and issues are not focused on individual students in the class but rather are attributed to a stereotype or public figure, students can express their own ideas and act out their true feelings without the risk of sanctions or reprisals, because they are "pretending" to feel like, think like, and act like another person. Simulations have an added advantage over traditional teaching methods in that they facilitate greater spontaneity of ideas and feelings, and more individual insights into the cause-and-effect relationships of events, into the dynamics of human behavior, and into the place of rules and standards in human conduct.

For instance, classroom simulations of prejudice in various forms may lead to a greater understanding of the nature of bigotry and to some workable recommendations for minimizing or preventing it. Simulations of political events, political decision making, international crises, arrest, trial, and appeal procedures, and legislative processes can also be examined in the classroom. Such simulations may not reduce every conflict or solve every problem students face, but they may give each student more insight and skills for interacting competently with his environment. He may come to recognize that the conflicts and problems others have are in some ways his own and that his decisions and behavior always affect the lives of other people.

Reality-oriented approaches can be devised to make every subject more relevant and interesting to learn. This means, however, that each subject—whether mathematics, economics, English, foreign languages, or science—must be defined not as a structure of knowledge to be imparted to students, but as a tool or way that helps students better understand and cope with their world. The teacher must extricate himself from the intricacies of the discipline and zero in on its fundamental use—a tool to help people communicate, find meaning in their lives, and develop the skills to cope with the problems of change and conflict.

Mathematics, the big bugaboo, can be learned effectively and enjoyably when students engage in reality-oriented activities such as exploring the practical uses of money and building model roads, towns, towers, canals, sewer systems, and so on. For example, an elementary-grade teacher can have his students arrive at some notion of the amount of money they would need to support themselves for a month or a year, just for the basic necessities—food, clothing, and shelter. Newspapers could be consulted to determine from the classified ads and the store prices the average monthly cost for a furnished room, for food, for clothing and laundry, and so on. The students could visit a local department store or use a catalogue to find out how expensive "little" things are, how realistic their initial proposed budget was, and how the cost of living goes up every year. Various math skills—computation, percentages, graphing—could be used to deal with related questions and problems (39). See Appendix B for available mathematics games.

Mathematics can also be used to describe students' physical characteristics and to measure their behavior under different conditions (77). For example, students can begin by measuring simple physical characteristics of themselves such as weight, height, and arm length, and gradually work out ratios such as height/weight and running speed/leg length and display them on charts and graphs. With a measuring tape they can work out height/age ratios for their class and other classes. Students can also estimate time without a watch, e.g., thirty seconds or one minute, and over successive trials determine how they can make their estimates more accurate. (Their classmates can use a stopwatch against which they can check the estimates.) They can measure blood pressure, respiration rate, and pulse rate under conditions of lying down, sitting, standing, walking, and running. They can find correlations between these different results, e.g., whether or not the fastest runners are the slowest breathers when respiration rate is measured at rest in a prone position. Various kinds of charts and graphs can be designed to display the correlations found. The learning of math skills in such a context becomes relevant to students and occurs more efficiently and rapidly.

Perhaps the most useful tools for helping students at the primary level learn the abstractions of mathematics through concrete manipulatable experiences are the Cuisenaire Colored Rods. These rods are stained pieces of wood from one to ten centimeters in length, with the length determined by the basic color pigments, e.g., white = 1, red = 2, yellow = 5, brown = 8 centimeters. With the rods, students can easily learn mathematical vocabulary and explore concepts of space and relationship such as: over, beside; big, bigger, biggest; tall, taller, tallest; small, short; first, second, third. If the teacher places the rods on a low table and gives students complete freedom to explore, measure, compare, build, tear down, and rebuild, he will observe how they discover concepts of space and relationship. He will hear a comment such as, "See how four red rods make one brown rod." With Cuisenaire rods students can eventually move to more complicated mathematical operations such as multiplication, division, and fractions.

Since most students benefit from a variety of mathematical tools and mathematically oriented activities, Dienes Multibase Arithmetic Blocks, Rasmussen worksheets, mirror cards, flannel boards, the abacus, bead frames, pool games, house building, and other related materials and activities can also be used. (*Grade Teacher* and *Instructor* often have useful suggestions on how to make mathematics and other subjects relevant to youngsters.)

Reality-oriented activities can also be planned when the boundaries of traditionally separate subjects are broken down and students can cut across subjects to explore, discover, and search for new meanings. As noted in Chapter 1, we do not in actuality learn or behave in terms of isolated ideas or feelings or experiences. Perceptions, ideas, feelings, and values from many different sources are interrelated to direct our behavior. Consequently, students need to be provided with opportunities to consider and work with all kinds of ideas and methods from different subjects, and to search for new relationships and meanings that may help them make some sense out of what they have experienced, what they are now concerned about, and what they can undertake next. For example, art, music, literature, and social studies can be integrated in the classroom to promote understanding of ethnic-group life styles and to explore solutions to social problems. Economics, art, and mathematics can be integrated to study the structure and organization of cities and how to build more desirable urban living conditions.

The same kind of open-ended explorations can take place within a single subject. In art, this would mean giving students the opportunity to paint and draw with a variety of media—

crayon, pastel, watercolor, india inks, colored inks, ballpoint pens, plain and colored pencils, charcoal, tempera, acrylics—to find out what it is they can do with the material at hand; to try out the medium on different sizes and shapes of different papers so that they discover something about the relatedness of form, function, and material; to create mosaics, using their imaginations as to what materials they might use (glass, stone, seeds, straw, feathers, macaroni, dried fruits, flowers, shells, grass, fur, buttons, string, bark, bottle caps, sponge, wood shavings, wood chips, styrofoam chips, plastic, cellophane, pebbles, steel wool, dried seaweed, netting); to work on designs, figures, landscapes; to create small or large murals or decorations for the classroom from almost anything (colored construction paper, pictures from magazines or newspapers, tissue paper, fabric, typing paper, wallpaper, Christmas cards, cereal boxes); and so on (72).

In a writing class, an open-ended approach might be to encourage each student to write about his personal experiences; to write about his home and family; to write about colors, words, tastes, moods, and how he senses different things in his environment when blindfolded—e.g., hair, velvet, bread, grass, sandpaper; to write a story that has no ending; to write a story that will never end; to write a story that has only one word.

Open-ended explorations of ideas, feelings, and methods in any subject provide relevance to students with different concerns and goals and kindle the search for new meanings.

Reality-oriented experiences can also be provided when students engage in honest and systematic inquiry into all of the issues and problems relevant to the subject at hand (92). Unfortunately, the opportunities to engage in such inquiry are rarely made available to students, because teachers assume that their subject areas need to be covered as comprehensively as possible, thereby allowing very little, if any, time for students to ask questions. It is agreed that all students must acquire competency in reading, writing, speaking, and working with information and symbols, but there is no such agreement about "organized bodies of knowledge" that are essential for all. In our rapidly changing society, it is impossible to predict what knowledge will be most useful or valuable to youngsters in the years ahead, and what new discoveries and developments will call for yet unthought-of responses. This suggests that teachers need not cover increasing amounts of subject matter but should instead help students acquire skill in identifying and dealing with changing knowledge. Personal and social problems will not be solved by requiring students to assimilate more and more subject matter that will be less and less applicable in years to come. They will be solved only when teachers help students analyze, evaluate, and actively try to solve each of the problems before them.

If students are to acquire meanings and competencies that will not betray them in the future, and if they are to become resourceful and creative individuals who will help solve rather than add to social problems, then honest, free, and thorough inquiry and discourse must be on the agenda of each classroom teacher. The search for meaning and competence must continually enable each student to state his doubts, questions, feelings, and values on the issues before him; to explore and discuss all possible implications of his views and proposed behavior for himself and others; to conceptualize the most plausible ways of interacting competently with his environment; to implement what seem to be the most effective, valid, or moral alternatives; and to evaluate the relevance and effectiveness of his decisions and actions. Such is the process of learning to deal constructively and responsibly with the realities of oneself and one's environment (92).

The preceding discussions suggest not only that reality-oriented activities make learning relevant but also that the student *can* conduct his search for meaning and competence as a whole person. More specifically, there are at least eight advantages in planning reality-oriented activities in the classroom regardless of whether they deal with history, race relations, budgeting money, supply and demand, reading, statistics about the body's structure and functions, art, or writing:

1. Reality-oriented activities and experiences can help the student develop the constructive attitudes and skills he needs to grapple with the whole range of real-world events and issues.

2. Reality-oriented activities, especially simulations in social studies and group behavior, can provide for the development of self-discipline more than most other forms of learning because of the built-in necessity of following rules, sharing, and cooperating to find a solution. Students become socially responsible through observing rules that are not arbitrarily imposed but that arise from the realistic learning activities they themselves have designed.

3. Reality-oriented activities can provide students with immediate and continuous appraisals of their behavior and progress. Each student, by his own actions, knows when he has learned and what he has learned. When a student makes a decision or takes a position or produces something, it has an immediate effect. Progress appraisals are natural. The student is therefore likely to perceive more meaningfully the consequences of his behavior and the reason for his progress or difficulties. Accordingly, the teacher can avoid the role of judge, and be a helper to the student.

4. Reality-oriented activities can enhance motivation more than most other approaches to learning because they are managed by students and based on their concerns. Students are not lectured to by teacher and textbook, and assembled to be tested and graded. Students, not teachers, make things happen.

5. Reality-oriented activities can help the student develop useful problem-solving skills more than any other learning approach. While the objective of reality-oriented activities may be to help students learn about the laws of supply and demand, the meaning of civil rights, the problem of pollution, or the operation of multiplication, each activity is designed in the form of questions, problems, or issues that the *student* has selected and must handle. Many skills are called into use—analytic, mathematical, intuitive, and so on. Moreover, once an answer or solution has been found, the steps followed in arriving at it can be reviewed and analyzed.

6. Reality-oriented activities can stimulate creativity and self-actualization by encouraging students to explore any idea, perception, or feeling, and to apply what they have learned to new or closely related situations, events, or problems.

7. Reality-oriented activities can help each student learn about the lives of other students and the lives of adults. They thus begin to recognize the interdependence and consequences of their behavior and the motives they and others have in behaving the way they do. The understanding that the students gain about themselves and others through this approach will help them to clarify their own values and will pave the way for constructive, self-directed behavioral change.

8. Finally, reality-oriented activities, regardless of the subject or materials used, will help the teacher and students discover that in any group each individual is a valuable resource for learning —that each person has a reservoir of experience and many useful skills—and that together they can help each individual to style his own development while at the same time contributing to the resolution of the issues and problems that face the entire group.

Procedures for Planning Reality-oriented Learning Programs

In a shared classroom the teacher and student assume equal responsibility for selecting and organizing learning programs. One of the teacher's important roles as coplanner is to help each student clarify his goals and consider the different kinds of learning programs that would help him achieve them. The teacher does this primarily through the use of relevant questions, suggestions, and materials. However, the teacher must not make the mistake of thinking that, in order to share planning in his classroom, he simply gathers his students together and asks them questions such as, "Students, what do you want to study?" or "What do you believe we should do as a class?" Students confronted with questions like these most likely will not be able to clarify their goals and consider appropriate alternative learning programs. Some students will be silent, others may respond dutifully with a long list of activities that they think the teacher wants them to complete, and still others may suggest activities that have little or no relevance to the subject. In any case, the teacher will find such a procedure ineffective. Unfortunately, many teachers have tried this approach or a similar one and, upon failing to achieve the desired results, have become convinced that students cannot assume any significant role in planning and directing their own learning (93).

Each student does not arrive in the classroom with all of his goals already neatly defined. Moreover, many students have not had *any* experience in making their own selections. Consequently, the teacher must help each student discover where he wants to go and how he wants to get there. The teacher can set the planning process in motion by offering suggestions to each student based on the information gathered and placed in his learning folder. However, in providing suggestions, the teacher must continually guard against manipulating students' ideas and preferences so that their learning programs become the teacher's programs. Planning should not be a game in which the teacher continues to make "suggestions" until students eventually propose to do what the teacher wants them to do. This is not an uncommon practice with teachers who claim to be democratic. An example of this practice is found in the following dialogue between a teacher and her students as they plan an outline for the study of homes (109):

PUPIL: Let's talk about problems connected with the home.
TEACHER: Start with a general outline first. A discussion of problems can come last.
PUPIL: Start with the first types of home and then work our way up.
TEACHER: What are the first things we should discuss before we take up types of homes?
PUPIL: Problems.
TEACHER: Let's leave a discussion of "problems" to the last.
PUPIL: Let's start with cave men and why they built homes.
TEACHER: Remember the outline. How shall we word it for the outline?
PUPIL: The reason for homes.
PUPIL: Let's discuss "What do you think of home?"

TEACHER: We're off the point.
PUPIL: We can discuss architecture, the architecture of long ago and of today.
TEACHER: What is our aim? Is it to discuss architecture?
PUPIL: Our aim is to study homes, then and now.
TEACHER: Yes, but what is our real aim?
PUPIL: How to improve the home.
TEACHER: That's right, improvement, not architecture.
TEACHER: What are the three words we think of when we use the word "comparison"?
PUPIL: Past, present, future.
TEACHER: Those weren't the words we used when we took up "schools."
PUPIL: The eighteenth, nineteenth, and twentieth centuries.
TEACHER (to rest of group): She left something out.
PUPIL: Colonial times.
TEACHER: What shall we do first?
PUPIL: Olden times.
TEACHER: Remember our study of the school. What comes first?
PUPIL: The necessity for homes.
TEACHER: What comes first under "homes"?
PUPIL: Responsibility. Each person's responsibility in the home.
TEACHER: No. First, the history of the home. Then, the reasons for the home. [Pp. 258–59]

The above process of classroom planning differs very little from authoritarian planning by the teacher. In fact, when a teacher worms and prods until his students adopt his program outline, including the specific wording that he planned before the class began its deliberations, he may be behaving in a more destructive manner, with his deceit and dishonesty, than the teacher who simply issues orders.

Some teachers deny students the right to participate in so subtle a manner that sometimes even they themselves do not know what is happening. Other teachers know very well what they are doing, but they would like their students to believe that they are working in a completely democratic manner. They may do this by limiting materials from which students can make selections to those areas they wish to cover. They may do it by the amount of enthusiasm they show when different activities and topics are mentioned. They may describe how a previous class engaged in an "extremely important" activity and speak so glowingly of the advantages found in that activity that the students become convinced that the same activity is also the best one for them (93).

In a shared classroom, the role of the teacher in planning is not to manipulate each student, but to help him make choices and pursue goals according to his sense of himself. In planning together with students, the teacher keeps the door open to listen to all the students' concerns, to draw out all suggestions about possible goals and activities, and to ask students to evaluate them. Constructive criticism and suggestions are to be given by the teacher, but not for the purpose of controlling each student's selections.

The following dialogue shows one way a teacher and students may plan together in a shared classroom (166). The example is a seventh-grade, combined English and social studies class for which no specific goals or activities have been established.

TEACHER (*sitting in circle with group*): Today we are going to begin planning some activities we might carry out during the time we are together. You know in this class you are going to help me to decide what we shall work on and how we shall go about our work. I am not going to tell you each day that certain things must be done as we go along, but rather we are going to decide together what would be best and most interesting for all of us. In other words, we will all share in the planning of our work. Let's suppose that this is a club that is meeting together for the first time. What might be the first step the club members would take to get their work under way?

STUDENT: Well, in our citizenship club in the sixth grade we had officers. We chose a president and a treasurer and some others to take charge of things.

TEACHER: I see. And do you think that is a good way to run a club?

STUDENT: Yes, I do. It gives the kids a chance to run things by themselves.

TEACHER: What do the rest of you think of Stanley's idea? Would you like to elect officers in this group and operate somewhat as a club might operate?

*(General consensus follows through the medium of
low mumbling of approval, nodding of heads, etc.)*

TEACHER: Suppose we begin, then, by electing a president or chairman. When we have chosen him we can decide whether we will need other officers and how we should go about electing them. What are some of the rules for electing a person to an office?

*(A discussion follows that brings out procedures for
nominating and voting as well as a review of the
qualifications necessary for holding such an office. . . .)*

TEACHER: How would it be if I would write the names of the nominees on the board so that no one will be left out. . . . Then someone can come up and write down the number of votes as they are counted.

(The election proceeds.) [Pp. 19–20]

In this brief interaction, the teacher makes it clear that she is not going to be the one to make all the decisions, but that everyone will share in selecting and planning classroom activities. She stresses the fact that she and the students will work together, thus including herself as a member of the group. She asks the students how they could proceed and then she acts on their suggestions, assuming the responsibility for getting things under way. She recognizes that it may sometimes take her and her students several hours to do cooperatively what she could do in a few minutes, but if she wants her students to free themselves to learn, and to learn to use freedom constructively and achieve lasting gains in self-discipline and self-responsible behavior, she needs to provide for joint planning and decision-making.

There is no single procedure that is appropriate for planning all programs with a group of students. Sometimes it is advantageous to develop long-range plans with the whole group and then let individuals and small groups work out the details—making daily plans for some areas of study, weekly plans for other areas, and other plans for special occasions. Sometimes it is appropriate to make only short-term plans because of students' changing interests. However, regardless of the planning techniques followed, the teacher and students must arrive at goals, activities, materials, and processes that are mutually agreeable.

A general procedure that the teacher and students may find
workable is to draw up a list of possible skill-developing activities that both believe are relevant and valuable to do. The teacher
helps by preparing in advance and distributing to students his
own list of activities that he believes touches on each of the important competency areas in the subject, yet allows students to
explore various areas in other subjects as well. The teacher's list
might be prefaced with a statement such as:

> To help you arrive at some decisions about the different kinds of
> activities you may wish to conduct, whether the activities are in-
> quiry sessions, simulations, or other skill-developing experiences,
> I have listed a number of sample activities below. You need not
> select any of these activities; they are simply suggestive of the
> different kinds of activities you may choose. However, the activity
> you choose must bear directly on a question, issue, or skill area
> in this subject or closely related areas, since at present we are not
> free to discard the time–subject-block approach to education.

The teacher and students would then consider each suggested
activity on each list and, remembering the students' concerns and
skills and the general goals to be achieved in the subject, select
or devise activities that seem most relevant for them to pursue over
the next two- or three-week period. The list would be updated
at the beginning of each week or whenever necessary, and students
would also be asked to suggest new activities when each activity
is completed and skills have been acquired.

It may be helpful and perhaps necessary in some classes for
the teacher also to provide students with some basic rules for
selecting activities (166). For example, the teacher may suggest
that each new activity should not only be relevant to the general
subject under consideration but should be related in some way
to a recently completed activity. In situations where the teacher
tries to engage the entire class in selecting a class activity, he
may find that all students are not in agreement. What happens if
the class cannot decide upon any one activity? How does the
teacher satisfy the minority group? Can the class work on more
than one activity at a time?

The solution to such a problem is provided by the situation itself. Since there are many phases to any given activity, the teacher can explore with the dissenting students how work on a particular phase might interest and challenge them. However, the teacher must not make the mistake of *requiring* the entire class to complete activities that are selected by the majority, but not by all of the students. Majority rule is a simplistic and often dangerous procedure to follow in coming to decisions, since it often leaves minority concerns and feelings unresolved. It is a win–lose method in which the majority of the students go away the happy winners and the remaining students go away the sad and hostile losers. History reminds us that when we make decisions by majority rule without dealing adequately with the concerns and feelings of minority groups, apathy, alienation, withdrawal, and violence are possible outcomes. Consequently, we must employ decision-making procedures that lead to mutually agreeable solutions. In the classroom this means that the teacher must help students deliberate in ways that allow all of them to plan activities acceptable to the entire class. When no agreement can be reached on a single group activity, then several closely related activities can be pursued simultaneously.

Defining the different possible phases of an activity is desirable not only because it helps the entire class discover how it can participate in a group endeavor, but also because it helps clarify for students how the phases of an activity are interrelated and what sequence would be appropriate for completing each phase. A learning activity in mathematics at the upper elementary level may initially read: "Construct a cardboard model of the Houston Astrodome based on its height, diameter, circumference, and cubic feet of space." In this case, the students and teacher may find it beneficial to break this activity into activity segments such as the following:

First Activity Segment
Obtain information about the exact height, diameter, and circumference of the Houston Astrodome through photographs, sketches, written descriptions, et cetera.

Second Activity Segment
Make a pencil drawing of the cardboard model of the Houston Astrodome on graph paper.

Third Activity Segment
Gather the materials needed to make the cardboard model and group them according to the sequence of steps to be followed in assembling the model.

Fourth Activity Segment
Assemble the model materials according to planned steps.

If this is to be a class project, each activity segment could be divided into specific tasks so that each student could have a particular role and responsibility in the project.

Initially, more than one class meeting often needs to be set aside for students to learn how to consider, select, and plan each of the different activities and activity segments that they would like to conduct. In time, however, they will be able to make decisions and fairly complete plans in a relatively short time.

Another procedure the teacher will want to consider in helping students plan and conduct reality-oriented classrooms is one applicable to simulations. The teacher might ask the class to suggest any problem or issue related to the subject that they think can be dramatized. The issue or problem may be a real-life situation or a fictitious example of a real situation. Suggestions may also develop from interpersonal problems that students have experienced in or out of the classroom. In any case, the situation should be concrete and real enough for students to understand its relevance.

In order to help students make some relevant selections, the teacher should prepare and distribute his own list of events or problem-situations that might be simulated. When making selections, the teacher and students need to keep in mind that the purpose of a simulation is more than the conveying of facts. It must deal with a reality-oriented conflict or problem involving differences of ideology, values, attitudes, feelings, or problem-solving strategies. Consequently, the teacher and students need to ask themselves during the selection process: "Does the situation involve a significant degree of conflict or controversy? Is the situation one that cannot be as adequately examined in inquiry sessions or through reading?"

If the teacher and students are using simulations for the first time, they should start with situations that are familiar and non-threatening and ones in which the action is clear cut. Gradually the class can explore delicate, emotion-laden situations (22).

Once a problem or situation has been selected, the teacher and students need to determine the objectives to be achieved from the simulation, the major and minor roles to be assumed by class members, the major events that are to take place and their sequence, and the rules the students can use as guides for displaying extemporaneous attitudes, feelings, lines of reasoning, and behavior during the simulation. Decisions on all these items would be arrived at jointly by the teacher and students through class discussion after they have researched various scenarios and roles related to the problem or situation selected. All information essential for conducting the simulation should be prepared on a ditto master, and, on the day before the planned simulation, each student should receive a dittoed copy of the scenario, individual profiles, rules, et cetera.

Another important point to note about conducting simulations is that the teacher and students have a responsibility to ensure the personal security and privacy of each individual involved, especially when reenacting interpersonal problems. The focus should be on issues of a general nature and not on individual and personal inadequacies or fears or on situations that are highly threatening. In all circumstances a student should feel free to decline a role if he feels uncomfortable in it. Even if a simulation session has been specifically designed to help a particular group of students, it may be better to involve them as observers rather than as active participants. Similarly, if the teacher feels that a recent classroom event offers an excellent opportunity for the class to explore an important issue or problem, it may be better to have the students who are directly involved in the problem be observers in the simulation before they become actors. They are thus insulated from a direct and possibly explosive confrontation, they can see how others might have handled the problem, and they can begin to look at their own behavior more realistically and draw their own conclusions about how such a problem can be competently handled. Later, as actors, they might be better able to face up to and learn to cope with their problems (22).

It is not an easy task for the teacher to prepare himself and the class to conduct simulations. Skill in helping others plan and conduct effective simulations cannot be acquired in private but only through interaction with others. One way the teacher can get practice and confidence is with friends, family, or colleagues. Perhaps several other teachers would like to learn how to plan and conduct simulations themselves and would agree to meet after school or in the evening. Often a small group of students will meet after school to help the teacher try out some simulated episodes as well as to suggest how simulations might be best developed for class. The teacher should also bear in mind that he and his students do not need to design all of their own simulations. There are many excellent simulations available commercially that can be adapted very well to issues or topics in economics, history, problems of democracy, sociology, social studies, and so on. (See Appendix B for an annotated list of available simulations and their publishers.) Also, the departments of education in many states often provide current and highly useful information about the availability and application of simulation games for the classroom. For example, the Bureau of General and Academic Education of the Pennsylvania Department of Education has a number of publications, including bibliographies and working papers, that can assist school administrators and teachers interested in using educational games. Titles currently available include: *Simulation Games for Social Studies, Games Assist Mathematic Education Success, Games Useful in Science Education, Environmental Education Games, A Laboratory Approach for the Teaching of Secondary School Mathematics.* Write: Division of Publications Distributor, Pennsylvania Department of Education, Box 911, Harrisburg, Pa. 17126.

A final point to note about designing or adapting simulations is that the selected activities must not be a series of unrelated classroom episodes or events. While a cardinal teaching rule is "Make classroom life relevant to the student's life," each student's learning program must be a series of interrelated experiences that move him toward the mastery of personally meaningful and socially constructive attitudes, concepts, and skills.

Another procedure that can be used to plan reality-oriented activities is one that is applicable when the teacher and students want to conduct group inquiry sessions on various ideas, issues, and problems in the subject (92). In planning inquiry sessions it is necessary to set aside a class meeting to draw up a list of the different kinds of topics, problems, and questions in the subject (or closely related to the subject) that the students feel are relevant to study at that time. The teacher can help with this planning procedure as with others by drawing up and distributing to students a list of topics that he knows are based in his field of study but that also relate to other subjects.

A second class meeting may be set aside for selecting the particular topics to be investigated. The teacher and students can take each topic on each of the lists they prepared the day before and individually accept, modify, or reject it. The final list of topics selected should reflect both the teacher's and students' best efforts to combine areas of investigation that they believe to be personally relevant and socially important. The order in which the topics will be examined and the amount of time to be allotted to the initial investigation of each topic also need to be decided. A schedule listing each of the topics and their respective dates and participants should be prepared and distributed to each student.

Often students disagree on some of the topics they wish to investigate. In these situations one or more multiple-topic sessions may be planned, with the different areas and their respective subgroups scheduled for the same inquiry session. It is advisable not to have a multiple-topic session until at least two or three other topics have been examined. This gives students an opportunity to develop an awareness of some of the procedures they need to follow to examine their topics effectively.

A useful way of helping students prepare for each separate inquiry session is to make relevant reading materials, taped lectures, and films accessible. This gives each student a chance to come in contact with a variety of information sources and reference points on which to base a discussion and helps him go beyond the text or his own past experiences in discussing an issue.

In short, the teacher's role in helping students plan inquiry sessions is to suggest a broad range of topics and the possible importance of each one to students, and to help students identify optional topics—topics that take into account the concerns, questions, and issues related to the subject. Beyond that, the teacher suggests materials, provides some of his own materials, helps students organize the topics, and helps them prepare a schedule for conducting inquiry into the specific topics selected (92).

Another technique that can be used to help each student plan activities in which he can participate meaningfully is to have the class number itself off at random so that students are organized in groups of five or six. Each group, with a teacher-appointed recorder, would meet for ten or fifteen minutes to select a general topic in the subject at hand and to draw up a list of the questions it would like answered. Following the meetings, each group would reports its questions to the entire class. The teacher would write them on the board or collect them and either assign a committee to prepare a list of questions or prepare a list himself. Each student would select two questions from the finished list and take two phases of a topic to investigate either by himself or with others (166).

One other aspect of planning classroom activities is important to note: often the processes of finding out where students are and planning reality-oriented learning activities may be combined. The teacher who takes students on a tour of the subject and then arranges "Teach Me" and "Tell Me" sessions is helping students plan while they are telling the teacher what some of their concerns are. Or, in their first class meeting, the teacher can assign each student a number in random fashion and then combine odd- and even-numbered students into pairs for five minutes, combine pairs into quartets for five minutes, and combine quartets into octets for ten minutes. Each subgrouping would have two tasks: (*1*) to share names, hobbies, interests, et cetera, and (*2*) to determine two or three things they especially want to learn, discuss, or experience about the subject. The teacher would already have prepared lists of inquiry topics and simulations and other skill-developing activities that students could use as aids in arriving at decisions (65).

Each octet would appoint a secretary to record the students' suggestions and preferences on a ditto master. The teacher would run off copies of each list—one from each octet—and distribute a copy of each list to each student at the second class meeting. For the first five minutes, each student would read through each list and make notes as further ideas occur to him. For the remainder of the second class meeting, the teacher would plan with the class the number and sequence of different activities they would like to perform, and the learning media, available resources, and methods of evaluation they would use.

The teacher would also make appropriate suggestions about lectures, demonstrations, projects, panels, committees, use of textbooks and supplementary written and visual materials, field trips, guest speakers, and the like. The teacher and the class may also find it helpful to invite a knowledgeable person from the staff to come in for half the period to help with the planning (e.g., the librarian, audiovisual director, curriculum director). Some people in the outside community could also be invited to offer the group their observations about the relevance of the group's goals and activities to the real world.

As the teacher and students set about the task of planning classroom activities, they may find that, regardless of the procedures they use, it is extremely helpful to have a planning checklist. The teacher could prepare a planning checklist and submit it to the students before they begin to formulate their plans. The primary purpose of a checklist would be to make the students think about available resources and about the most effective way of organizing activities (141). The planning checklist might include the following items:

1. What goals do we want to achieve?
2. Should we expect the entire class to achieve each of the goals?
3. What goals should be achieved by the total class? By small groups? By individual students?
4. Should some goals be achieved before other goals? Which ones?
5. What activities will help us achieve our goals?
6. Should some activities be completed before others are begun? What should be the sequence of the activities?
7. What are the major parts of each activity?
8. Are all parts of the activity equally essential? Can some parts of the activity be omitted if a difficulty arises? Which ones?
9. How much time is needed to complete each activity? How much time should be set aside to complete all of the activities? Should the schedule for completing all the activities coincide with the end of a grading period?
10. What skills are needed to conduct the activities?
11. Who in the class has the needed skills?
12. Are the needed skills ones that we can develop? How?
13. Does the teacher have the skills needed?
14. Which of the teacher's skills are to be used? How?
15. Should an "expert" be brought in? Who? When? How?
16. What resources do we need to conduct each of our activities?
17. What resources are available in class?
18. What resources can be brought to class or purchased by the students? By whom?
19. What resources can be constructed in class? By whom?
20. What resources can be brought to class or purchased by the teacher? How?
21. If a dispute arises over methods or the use of available resources, how will the dispute be resolved? What is the teacher's role?

In helping students plan, the teacher must keep in mind that the process of planning inquiry sessions, simulations, and other reality-oriented activities can become routinized and monotonous. Consequently, the teacher needs to help students learn how to design activities that incorporate their spontaneous ideas and feelings on a topic. He also needs to help them devise new variations in the format of planning and learn how to organize themselves into different groups and achieve several different goals simultaneously. For example, the teacher needs to help the class learn how to organize itself so that, when appropriate, one group can conduct an inquiry session while a second group conducts a simulation and a third group undertakes a problem-solving activity, all directly or closely related to a particular topic. The groups can also learn how to rotate the learning methods they use and share their discoveries or skills with each other.

The teacher who makes every effort to help students plan reality-oriented activities has the special responsibility of selecting relevant texts, references, and supplementary readings. The major concern in selecting reading materials is to determine whether or not they are designed to facilitate self-directed learning on the part of students (121). More specifically, the following questions may be a helpful guide when selecting texts:

1. Is the text adaptable to students who differ in their concerns, skills, and learning styles?
2. Does the text enable the student to do a variety of things?
3. Does the text enable students to learn from each other?
4. Does the text give students realistic opportunities to plan and conduct their own activities?
5. Does the text ask open-ended questions or does it ask questions with "right" answers?
6. Are the questions the text asks important to the students or to the teacher or to the author of the text?
7. Does the text encourage students to ask their own questions?
8. Does the text encourage students to challenge its statements?
9. Does the author of the text point out to the student what his particular biases are and what the other points of view and methods of finding answers are?

10. Is the text a recent edition that relies primarily on current reference works to provide students with ideas and suggestions?

If the available texts are in some respects unsatisfactory, the teacher may find it necessary to edit readings or write new reading materials. Often when the reading materials are current the only change needed is to make parts of the text lucid by paraphrasing the author's ideas without destroying his meaning or diluting the idea to a point where it is insulting to a student's intelligence. For example, D. Selakovich (143) describes how the essay "Why We Are Having a Wave of Violence" by James Wilson (*The New York Times Magazine,* May 19, 1968, pp. 23–24) was paraphrased in parts for easier comprehension in a social studies class:

> Wilson's use of the term "relative deprivation" became in the translated version: "poor in comparison with some of their neighbors," and the sentence: "Labor-management violence was in the nature of internal war between two organized opponents struggling over a quite tangible stake," became: "The main issue in the struggle between labor and the owners of certain industries was whether or not the union would be recognized." The idea was there, but the language was much simplified. Here and there, in the interpretation of language, the teacher found it easy and natural to place an abstract term in parentheses after its definition in the text. Thus, the phrase: "poor in comparison with some of their neighbors (relative deprivation)," was placed in the text. In later discussion the teacher did not dwell on the "correct" term nor was it emphasized on the examination. The idea was emphasized, not the term itself. [P. 102]

The overworked teacher may be tempted to dismiss this suggestion, but he will be surprised to find that some of the brighter students in his class and in other classes at his school can help in this activity. Mothers in some school districts will often assist with rewriting and editing reading materials.

One last point about reading materials: when considering the different kinds of supplementary readings to make available, the teacher will want to consult bibliographies that deal with a wide range of ethnic and social groups and their concerns and problems. Many excellent bibliographies are available from different organizations and publishers. *About 100 Books,* a bibliography on intergroup understanding, can be purchased for twenty cents from Division of Youth Services, The American Jewish Committee, 386 Fourth Avenue, New York, N.Y. 10016. *Personal Problems of Children* is available for ten cents from Campbell and Hall, Inc., 989 Commonwealth Avenue, Boston, Massachusetts 02215. Perhaps the best sources of up-to-date reading materials for students are the directors of children's services of major metropolitan libraries and the American Library Association. For example, Augusta Baker, head of the Office of Children's Services at the New York Public Library, makes available a pamphlet with an extensive bibliography of current selections.

When all of the resources for learning have been organized and when each student has selected the program of activities he will complete, the teacher and student may design a "learning contract." If the class has not already discussed the rationale for employing learning contracts, the teacher may find it helpful to provide one such as the following:

> When the teacher and student enter into a joint venture, it is necessary for them to arrive at a mutual agreement regarding the responsibilities they will assume. One way of clarifying each person's responsibilities and the conditions under which they agree to complete classroom activities is to have the teacher and student enter into a written contract. The contract is designed to protect both the teacher and student from making unrealistic demands on each other and from making capricious changes in their goals. It obligates both of them to make realistic commitments to each other and to honor these commitments.

The learning contract should specify in simple and clear language the objectives to be achieved, the specific activities and activity segments to be completed, and the commitments that both the teacher and student have agreed to fulfill. Where appropriate, the teacher and involved students should also determine and state in the contract (*1*) the standards for recognizing when each activity has been satisfactorily completed, (2) the sequence in which the activities are to be completed, (3) the materials and equipment to be used, (4) the general duration of each activity and of the total program, e.g., two days or one week, (5) the tentative date on which materials or products are due, (6) the grade the student will receive for completing or failing to complete his planned learning program, e.g., A, B, C, or Incomplete, (7) the deadline for changing a learning contract.

When the learning activity involves a simulation, decisions need to be made jointly by teacher and students regarding (1) the individual players and groups involved, (2) the major interaction sequence among the players and the general objectives to be pursued, (3) the rules or guides each player will use to decide the general kinds of extemporaneous behavior or lines of thinking and feeling that he is free to explore during the simulation.

Copies of the learning contracts should be distributed to the involved students and placed in their learning folders so that both the students and teacher have a guide and a reference for keeping an accurate and complete record of each classroom transaction and for assessing progress. If a learning program involves the total class, the teacher can either place the learning contract on the blackboard or distribute a mimeographed copy of it to each student. Figure 3 provides an example of an individual learning contract that may be appropriate in some subject areas at the upper elementary and high school levels.

The teacher may find it necessary to include in the contract more detailed explanations of agreed-upon procedures. For example, under *Grades* he may prefer to include the following:

The grade you receive for each of your activities will be arrived at jointly by you and me. Immediately after completing each of your activities, you and I will share our observations about your performance and try to arrive at a mutually acceptable grade. If a dispute arises about the grade you believe you should receive, and we are unable to come to an agreement about your grade, you may ask a panel of your classmates, chosen at random (e.g., every other name on the class roster), or a grievance committee (if one exists) to review the matter and to recommend a grade. The grade

Figure 3.

<u>Individual Learning Contract</u> (Teacher's Copy)

I _____ agree to complete each of the following activities in
(student's name)

_____ during the period of _____.
(subject or field of study)   (dates)

I. <u>Readings, Inquiry Sessions, and Examinations</u>
    (if applicable)

    I agree to complete the following three readings by the dates
specified in preparation for either Option A or Option B below.

    <u>Readings</u>   <u>Date</u>

    1. _____   _____
    2. _____   _____
    3. _____   _____

    Check (✓) either A or B below.

( ) <u>Option A</u>
    I choose to participate in the group inquiry sessions that will
examine the topic _____ on the following days _____. I
agree to complete a brief written personal reaction on each of the
three readings listed above and to turn it in to the teacher before the
scheduled inquiry sessions begin.

( ) <u>Option B</u>
    I choose to complete the readings independent of the inquiry
sessions, and for each reading I agree to draw up and respond to five
open-ended questions that I feel are important to me and the topic.

II. <u>Projects, Simulations, and Skill Activities</u>
     (if applicable)

    I agree to complete the following projects, simulations, or
skill activities on the dates specified. (If with other students,
please use a Group Learning Contract.)
                                                    <u>Date</u>
    1. _____   _____
    2. _____   _____
    3. _____   _____
    4. _____   _____

III. Grades

I understand that the grade I will receive will be either A, B, C, or Incomplete, depending on the extent to which I complete my learning program and on the level of competency I achieve in each activity.

I wish to work for the grade _____, and according to my
(A, B, or C)
agreement with the teacher this requires that I demonstrate the following levels of achievement _____.
(write in as agreed to by you and the teacher)
I understand that if I am dissatisfied with the grade I receive from the teacher for my efforts, I may appeal to my classmates for a final decision.

IV. Program Change

I understand that if I am unhappy with the progress I am making in my learning program I may ask to have my entire program or parts of it modified on or before _____ if such modifications will make better
(date)
use of my concerns and skills.

_____   _____
(date)   (student's signature)

_____   _____
(date)   (teacher's signature)

Note: Please sign and date both copies of your learning contract when you have filled them out, and have the teacher sign both copies and return the "student copy" to you. Both copies of your learning contract must be filled out and signed on or before _____.
(date)

that the panel or committee recommends and the two grades that you and I recommend will be averaged to determine your activity grade.

Since the entire class should know what is going to happen during the days for which plans have been made and what part the students and the teacher will play, it may also be appropriate for the class to organize all of the learning programs, goals, and decisions into a flow chart for the period planned and display it in class.

After the learning contracts have been filled out and distributed and a flow chart has been prepared and displayed, the teacher and students may find it helpful to discuss how they feel about the joint planning experience. The teacher may wish to prepare and administer a short reaction sheet, e.g., "How We Planned," as a basis for analyzing their decision-making processes. Although it is unlikely that the students will have done anything like a perfect job of planning, the planning experience and the follow-up analysis should be a giant step toward helping students learn how to plan effectively for self-directed learning.

A final point about planning: the teacher must recognize that a student's interests may change markedly before he completes his planned learning program. This is especially true at the primary level, where interests arise and wane or develop in many different ways. Moreover, a student's interests inside the classroom change because of the interplay between in-school and out-of-school learning. Learning does not end when the student leaves the classroom or school for the day. The student will go home or to the playground or into some other setting that will be influenced by the day's classroom events. His out-of-class experiences in turn will influence what he can and wants to do the next day in the classroom. He comes to school each day seeking continuity in his learning. He wants classroom life to tie together with his currently perceived needs and expectations about his immediate future outside the classroom. Consequently, he must be permitted to explore and pursue unplanned activities and topics in the classroom.

The teacher will find that it is not possible to predict all or even most of the activities that will provide a student with continuity in his search for meaning, competence, and his sense of himself on a particular day. For example, while a student is reading about an adventure he may become interested in discussing how to survive on an island without prepared rations, or in discovering why volcanoes erupt, rather than in finding out what happened to the hero in the adventure. Or while studying the Constitution or the Bill of Rights, students may become interested in their rights as students or in fair grading policies. A topic in mathematics may lead students to examine how different gambling procedures operate—what the probabilities are of winning at dice, poker, roulette, and so on. While studying how Congress functions, students may become involved in a discussion about how to pass laws that protect consumers and minors. As Herbert Kohl points out in *The Open Classroom* (87), in order for the teacher to provide continuity, he must put aside his preferences and expectations and go with the class—respond to the students' ideas about using materials and solving problems and not cut off their enthusiasm in the service of getting through all the planned activities. Consequently, the teacher must always be ready to modify students' learning programs and even permit the students to set aside their learning programs temporarily to make good use of their newly acquired concerns and to take advantage of rare learning opportunities.

However, each student must still be required to complete a learning program. The teacher must always seek a balance between the student's need to explore new concerns and his obligations to fulfill his agreement to complete an individual learning program or to contribute to a group project.

Let me summarize what I believe are the important points about the process of planning classroom learning events:

The teacher does not dictate to the student what his learning program will be, nor does the student arbitrarily select the goals and activities he will pursue. The planning process is a joint enterprise involving the teacher and student. The basic role of the teacher is to uncover, suggest, and clarify the range of reality-oriented learning opportunities open to each student in view of his current concerns and skills, the nature of the subject, the available materials, and the social context of the classroom.

When a total learning program has been agreed upon jointly, the teacher and student may draw up a learning contract. The teacher recognizes that when students freely commit themselves to completing a learning program, they must be held accountable for their decisions. If the capability to engage in self-directed learning is to be successfully developed, the student must not be excused from his commitment. The teacher makes it clear that free choice is conditional: with freedom to choose, there is accountability for choices. If the student fails to uphold the terms of his commitment, he runs the risk of being denied equal voice in selecting and planning future learning programs.

The teacher also recognizes that many important details of any meaningful learning experience and often the basic direction of learning itself cannot be laid out in advance and remain authentic inside the classroom any more than it can outside the classroom. Consequently, an important rule the teacher sets for himself is to "roll with" the class and let students temporarily set aside a learning program when they suddenly become intensely involved in discovery in ways and directions other than those planned. The teacher and individual student or classroom group jointly work out program modifications while recognizing that a balance needs to be found between exploring new ideas and capitalizing on rare learning opportunities, on the one hand, and fulfilling commitments, on the other.

8

The Helping Relationship

IN ORDER TO achieve the goals of his learning program, the student needs to receive continuous and detailed information about the relevance and effectiveness of each of his learning strategies. He needs to know at any given point whether or not he should retain or modify his current learning approach. If he needs to change his present strategy, the teacher must help him plan and employ a more effective one.

The teacher can discover the necessity of providing the student with continuous and detailed progress feedback by participating in the following experiment with a colleague or friend. Arrange two writing areas about five feet apart. Standing back to back, try to "teach" your friend how to draw the design in figure 4. He may not see the design, but must draw it only from the verbal directions you give him. Nor may you see his efforts to reproduce the design until you both decide to terminate the activity. When the session is over, compare his drawing with your design and ask him why he believes he was not able to do a better job. Ask yourself why his lines weren't placed more accurately. Discuss the different ways your role as a "teacher" could have been modified to ensure that your friend would have drawn a more accurate representation of the design. This experiment should

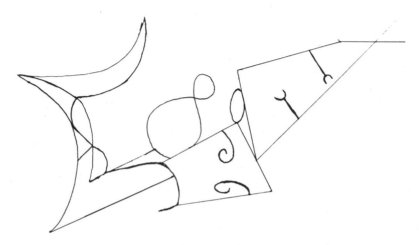

Figure 4.

serve to illustrate that a teacher would not be very helpful in facilitating learning if he waited until the *end* of an activity, or the *end* of a class period, or day, or week, to provide feedback to the student about his performance and the effectiveness of his learning strategies. Clearly, in order to make optimal progress in his learning program, a student needs to receive continuous and detailed information about the quality of his performance.

The teacher must bear in mind, however, that a successful helping relationship is established with a student only when progress feedback and guidance are defined in terms of their effects on the student and not in terms of the value the teacher places on them. This means that in making a decision about the kind and amount of help to give a student, the teacher needs to help the student verbalize his current level of awareness of each of the concepts and skills involved in his activity and to provide him with the cues he needs when he needs them. Obviously, the skill to be acquired or the goal to be achieved may suggest in part the kind and amount of help that the teacher needs to provide. For example, the goal to be achieved may be such that the teacher can be most useful to students when he helps them break down a task into several parts and, by his questions, helps them explore specific relationships or ways of making things happen. Alternately, a learning goal may be such that the only assistance students require is an occasional, thought-provoking question. However, while the goal itself may sometimes guide the teacher on how to help a particular student, he should make no assumptions about the amount and kind of assistance he needs to provide. The teacher should always rely on the student's rate of progress and his level of awareness of his situation when deciding the help to give him.

Two classroom dialogues of teachers engaged in helping relationships with students will serve to illustrate the importance of this approach. In the first classroom, high school students try to discover the chemical composition of a substance without tasting, touching, or smelling it (4).

STUDENT: It's water.

TEACHER: Lift it.

STUDENT (*lifting the sample*): It looks like water, but it's awfully heavy.

STUDENT (*inspecting the sample*): It's too heavy to be water.

STUDENT: I don't know any colorless liquids besides water.

STUDENT: What about alcohol?

STUDENT: Alcohol is lighter than water. What other substances are there?

STUDENT: Let's find some of its properties. We'll freeze some and boil some.

(*Later*)

STUDENT: It boils at 77°C., but we can't freeze it with ice. Do we have any dry ice?

(*Later*)

STUDENT: It freezes at about —22°C. Let's see if it will burn.

STUDENT: It might explode.

TEACHER: What if Karen is right? Get me a platinum wire. We'll try a little bit at a time.

STUDENT: Should we use the hood?

TEACHER: Oh, yes.

STUDENT: It doesn't burn.

STUDENT: Let's find out how heavy it is.

STUDENT: How?

STUDENT: Weigh a graduated cylinder then add 100 cc and weigh it again.

(*Later*)

STUDENT: It weighs 160 grams, so its density is 1.6 grams per ml., its melting point is −22°C., and it boils at 77°C. But I still don't know what it could be.

STUDENT: Let's add some water to it.

STUDENT: The water floats on top.

STUDENT: Try alcohol.

STUDENT: It dissolved. What else can we do?

TEACHER: You've discovered many of the descriptive properties of the substance. Someone smell it.

STUDENT: Whew! It's chloroform or something.

STUDENT: We'll look in the chemistry handbook to see if chloroform has the properties we've discovered.

STUDENT: It can't be chloroform. The freezing point is too high.

STUDENT: What is the formula for chloroform?

STUDENT: $CHCl_3$.

STUDENT: Chloroform isn't heavy enough. Can we replace the H with another chlorine? What is CCl_4?

STUDENT: It is CCl_4. Everything checks. Fairly closely, anyway. [Pp. 222–25]

In this activity the teacher discovered through observation how he could help his students succeed in their own way. He intruded only when a test became too dangerous or when a question or suggestion seemed necessary. He relied on their levels of awareness and patterns of responding to determine the kinds of questions to ask and suggestions to offer.

The same approach is also employed in the second dialogue, which is the culmination of six weeks of study by high school students about secret societies (100). Only portions of the dialogue are reproduced here.

RICHARD: I think that all violent secret societies sprang up in countries where people were oppressed by their governments.

DEBBIE: We could make up a rule for ourselves: If we hear of a violent secret society in a certain place or country, then we can say that there is an oppressive government there also.

ANNE: Many of the societies we studied fit in very well with our rule.

TEACHER: What if I asked you to prove your rule?

ANNE: Well, I could get examples of secret societies that fit our rule.

TEACHER: Well?

ANNE: For instance, the Serbian Black Hand was very violent, and helped bring about World War I. The Serbians and Yugoslavians were being oppressed by the Austrian government which seemed to want to make these areas part of its own Empire. The Serbs wanted to unite their people and free themselves from Austrian rule and pressure, so many Serbs joined the Black Hand to hurt the Austrians. . . .

JANET P.: Cuba might be an example of what we are looking for. Cuba was ruled by a dictator who the Communists overthrew. I read that that might be part of the reason Castro was so popular. He threw out their dictator, but then he put himself in the dictator's place.

STEVE: Yea, Communists are actually a kind of secret organization and they are for overthrowing governments.

JOHN: They were the ones that took Russia over. According to that speech we read by Lenin, they were secret, and they even thought the Russian government was made up of foreigners and was rotten and oppressive.

RUTH: Of course, in the United States the Communists are kind of quiet. They aren't openly violent here or even secretly violent. If they were, the FBI would catch them all and put them in jail.

ANNE: Our government isn't oppressive.

TEACHER: How do you know that all the other governments were oppressive?

ANNE: Well, in those countries the people had to resort to violence to get what they wanted, while here the people can talk openly about it, even the Communists, I think.

JAVIER: Why aren't there any secret societies in Russia now? We think their present form of government is oppressive and the people are not free there. There should be secret societies there.

JANET: We never hear of assassinations there, or street bombings like there are in Viet Nam. Maybe the Russians are peaceful because they have their *own* bad government and they are not being ruled by foreigners.

TEACHER: That's assuming they were ruled by foreigners before. Aren't you taking Lenin's word for that?

JANET: I suppose so.

STEVE: If we reverse our rule. . . . Let me see. . . . It will read differently. Uh . . . It will read that we should find secret societies where there are oppressive governments. But we don't in Russia. We don't hear of bombings, assassinations, revolts, or trouble there.

ANNE: Maybe they don't let you hear about it. . . .

STEVE: That could be, but how could they keep a big revolt quiet?

ALLEN: There was a revolt in Hungary . . . in, I think . . . 1956 or 1957 . . . anyway, they couldn't keep that quiet. I guess there was an underground in Hungary.

JOHN: That time the Russians would be the oppressors.

SHARON: Maybe you don't hear about these things in the newspapers, until one of the secret societies, or the underground, starts to act. You won't hear of these things because the bad government wants to keep it all quiet.

LAUREN: When the United States was oppressed, I think that there were secret organizations here too, to fight the British during our Revolutionary War. The British would be our oppressors.

JAVIER: They would sort of be foreigners, too. That seems to be important. Maybe people are less angry at being ruled, even badly, by their own countrymen, than by outsiders.

JANET: Our rule seems to hold pretty good. If we reverse it, we do seem to have some trouble, but that's because the proof is hard to find. It's easier to work after the fact, after something has already happened.

LAUREN: I just thought of a new problem. Maybe we're all being too agreeable with our own rule. We didn't consider the Ku Klux Klan. We studied it, and we have their oath, but where do they fit into our rule?

TEACHER: Ah! That is a very good question.

JANET P: They thought that the American government in Washington was being oppressive to the white people of the South, so they formed their organization to protect their rights.

TEACHER: I like your choice of words.

JANET P: What does that mean?

TEACHER: What do you think it means?

STEVE: Oh! I think I see what you're getting at. Janet said that the Ku Klux Klan *thought* the U.S. government was bad. But was it? For whom? It wasn't bad for the Negroes in the South. . . .

DEBBIE: No. It was giving the Negroes their rights for the first time. The KKK was oppressing the Negroes.

DONALD: The KKK obviously thought that the U.S. government was interfering with their old way of life, and, since they couldn't get their old life back legally, they resorted to violence and formed a sort of secret club to frighten Negroes and Northerners who came South.

ALLEN: They thought of Northerners as foreigners, and even called them all sorts of bad names.

DEBBIE: Maybe we should change our rule to read that there are violent secret societies when people *feel* that they are being oppressed by their government or some foreign ruler.

JAVIER: I guess it all really depends on what's in people's minds.

RICHARD: But couldn't there be something definitely labeled a bad government allowing no freedom?

LAUREN: But that's all according to the way we think. It really depends on what those people think. For instance, if most people in a country don't mind dictators, then you probably won't have any revolts or undergrounds. I don't think the French were so bad in Algeria or treated the Algerians so terribly, but the Algerian Moslems wanted to have their own country, so they formed secret terrorist groups and tried to force the French to leave.

RUTH: They succeeded, too.

DEBBIE: I guess we'll have to leave it that way—as feelings—and just keep looking for more proof. [Pp. 42–47]

Here, again, the teacher determined the kind of help he needed to provide from the ways in which the students perceived relationships and tested their perceptions. It is clear from both dialogues that, to establish a successful helping relationship, the teacher needs to provide the kinds of materials, questions, and suggestions that enable the student to develop his own answer-finding and problem-solving approaches, that help him to conceptualize and try out his own notions about what is true and what works. Again, the individual student's level of awareness of the concepts and skills involved and his rate and style of learning dictate the kind and amount of help he needs to receive at a particular point in his activity.

The teacher should also remember that learning is essentially an internal process. This means that, if he is to gather reliable information about the student's current level of awareness of the concepts and skills involved in his particular activity, the teacher needs to check with the student and find out how the *student* feels about his progress. He needs to ask each student at frequent intervals how he is doing, whether or not he needs or wants help, and, if he needs help, what kind of help he wants. This point is important also because each student wants to be independent at the same time that he wants and needs adult guidance and support. It is not ambivalence or disorganized behavior. He is simply saying, "I want to do it for myself, but I may not know the way at all times. Would you help me when and only when I ask for it?" He wants to feel that he has some control over the amount and kind of guidance he receives.

Our comments about establishing a helping relationship suggest unmistakably that if the teacher is to be an effective helper, he continually needs to evaluate the relevance and usefulness of his entire behavior as a teacher. He needs to determine whether or not his language level is appropriate for his students. If he is helping them master skills, he needs to determine whether or not the examples and demonstrations he is providing are simple and clear. He also needs to determine whether or not the skill or task is broken down into appropriate steps and whether the teaching sequence is consonant with the students' level of awareness and rate and style of learning. This last point is most important, especially when complex skills are being learned. The rule of taking only one step at a time in a complex learning sequence is based on the fact that the more steps the teacher takes, the greater the number of concepts and skills he introduces, and these in turn make it more difficult for the student to focus on the specific skills that need to be mastered first.

As a rule, if a student has difficulty at a particular point in the learning sequence, the teacher is asking him to take too many steps at one time. The teacher is asking the student to acquire what is for him a high-level skill or concept, involving the interplay of several lower-level skills or concepts that he has not completely mastered. When a student is having difficulty making progress, he is saying to the teacher, in effect, "You're asking me to learn too many things at once. Could you simplify it?" The teacher needs to find out where the hidden difficulty is. Maybe it's a word that the student doesn't understand. Maybe the teacher is moving too rapidly and not giving the student a chance to think things through. Maybe the performance involves procedures the student has not yet learned. Through a series of questions the teacher should backtrack and find out what the trouble is (37).

The teacher should always be alert as to whether the sequence, examples, demonstrations, or verbal cues are forcing a learner into using a style unnatural to him. If a rule-before-examples approach helps some students, the teacher should continue to use it with those individuals. But if others seem upset by this approach, the teacher should try an examples-before-rule method and other approaches to determine which work best for each student. The teacher must recognize and be able to provide the number of steps, step sizes, and kind and number of concrete illustrations each student needs to make satisfactory progress in his learning program. Further, the teacher must bear in mind that if a skill or concept is useful, it can be broken down and clearly demonstrated. However, if the teacher finds that he is unable to break down a complex concept or skill into simple enough learning segments, he should set it aside for the time being, since he can be of little help to the students in learning it at that point (37).

The suggestion of breaking down difficult concepts, principles, and skills into steps should not be interpreted to mean that the teacher will tell the student everything or even most things. After breaking down an activity or task into steps appropriate to the student, the teacher establishes a helping relationship primarily through posing questions that enable the student to move satisfactorily through his learning sequence and to acquire the skills or meanings in his own way.

Regardless of the learning to be achieved, the teacher does not control the student's thinking or behavior. For example, he does not take a first-grader's hand in his and push it around the paper in an effort to improve his drawings of squares and rectangles. Nor does he write out for a tenth-grader each of the steps for solving a geometry problem because "the student is taking too much time." This kind of "help" has doubtful value and may in fact interfere with the learning style that is emerging in the student. The first-grade teacher could instead sit down with the student and place one sheet of paper before the student and one before himself. He could then break down each geometric form into a number of simple lines and proceed to draw on his sheet one line at a time, asking the student after each stroke to see whether he could "do something like that" on his sheet. The teacher could draw increasingly more complex lines on his sheet until the student could draw each figure by himself. With the tenth-grader, the teacher could ask the student questions about the simple relationships involved in the problem and then, beginning where the student has some difficulty, ask questions about increasingly more complex relationships at whatever rate and with whatever supportive examples would help the tenth-grader learn how and why the geometry problem can be solved.

Each student must learn to acquire competencies and meanings himself. If he is a passive instrument, with the teacher at the controls, he gains nothing from the experience since, when he is required to deal with the issue, perform the skill, or solve the problem later on, he must rely on himself. The teacher may believe that he is speeding up the learning process when he does things for a student or tells him everything, but he is actually forcing the student to depend on the teacher and is cheating him out of learning in his own way (37).

This point is important to keep in mind not only when the teacher is helping the student acquire useful skills, but also when he is conducting inquiry sessions, i.e., when each student is searching for answers, attitudes, and values that make sense to *him*. If the teacher simply tells a student the "right" way of viewing events or of feeling toward people, or if the teacher uses a set of sequential statements to get a student to zero in on the answers that are important only to the teacher, the student's search for meaning and competency becomes a phony one. Inquiry learning is not a game in which the teacher says, "Here is something I know that I think is important; now let's see if you know it." Rather, in honest inquiry the teacher says to the student, "This is a controversial issue; I would like to know what you think about it and I will respect any position you take on it." The teacher must help the student to pursue any aspect of an issue he wishes and to arrive at his own answers and solutions on the basis of reliable evidence and persuasive argument. The teacher must help the student recognize that there are no "right" or "wrong," "good" or "bad" answers, but only more or less workable, plausible, and defensible ones (92).

Since the kind of help needed varies tremendously from student to student and from activity to activity for the same student, the teacher must be able to employ a wide range of thought-provoking questions to facilitate progress and mastery. At times the teacher may need to ask the student to consider the consequences of following through with something ("What would happen if——?"). At other times the teacher may ask him to compare ideas or situations ("What do they have in common?"). He may ask the student to evaluate evidence ("Why do you feel that this statement is true?"), to look for a conclusion ("What do these particular observations suggest to you?"), to explain something ("Why do you feel that would apply in this instance?"), or to test an idea ("How might you check your notion out?"). The teacher must also be able to parlay his questions, and help the student explore the mechanisms of his past learning and consider whether or not these mechanisms are in some way applicable to his present situation. For example: "Have you encountered this kind of problem before? . . . Good! How is this problem different from that problem? . . . Fine! What additional facts do you believe you need to know? . . . Very good! What do you believe is the next step to take? . . . Sounds good, give it a try!"

Since each student needs to feel that his individual efforts, interpretations, and feelings are valued and that the teacher will not criticize his responses or work, the teacher's questions should be exploratory in nature, eliciting the student's personal impressions rather than requiring "right" answers. For example, questions such as "What did you find interesting in the readings?" or "How meaningful were the situations in the film to you?" are exploratory in nature rather than judgmental. The teacher's questions should also convey a desire to understand as do these: "Could you elaborate on that a little more?" "How may that recommendation be applied to our situation?" "Do you feel that this suggestion would solve the entire problem or just some aspects of it?" "Would a different approach to the problem be more effective?" "What may be some of the implications of this plan for each person's behavior?" "What might be some of the workable aspects of that suggestion?" (92).

After posing a question, the teacher must let the student figure out his own way of doing things. He does not require the student to agree with him or with other students, nor does he try to reach a compromise every time there is a difference of opinion. He should view controversy as a powerful motivating device, he should encourage different views, and he should help his students consider the different ways they can explore an issue or solve a problem.

If the teacher finds that a student is unresponsive to a question he has raised, he needs to determine whether or not the student is afraid to answer, or does not understand the question, or views the question as unimportant. Consequently, the teacher continually needs to ask himself about the appropriateness of his questions: Are the questions judgmental and threatening? Are they clear and understandable? Are they vague or too general? Am I posing a question that incorporates other questions that should be posed individually? Moreover, when a teacher is explaining something, he should never say more than a few sentences without asking a question to determine whether or not he is being understood and whether or not what he is saying is useful to the students.

Although the teacher should never use threatening statements or questions, he needs to help students become critical thinkers when conducting inquiry sessions. When the sessions are far enough along and students have developed considerable trust in the teacher and confidence in themselves, the teacher can press them to present more evidence and logic for each of their responses and to defend each important generalization or assumption they make. An example of a teacher's statement that requires the student to defend his position is: "I think I understand what you are saying; however, I can't seem to reconcile your position with the fact that——." It must be remembered, however, that student self-confidence and the trust that often takes so long to develop between a student and teacher can be quickly chipped away by negative statements and threatening questions (92).

Further, when a student receives a negative comment from his classmates, the teacher should not allow it to go unchallenged. The teacher should use the comment to demonstrate that he has faith in the struggling student. For example, if a student says, "Billy is a dummy," the teacher should make it clear that name-calling is out of order and that "Billy is quite smart. Billy will get it right and that will show us that he *is* smart." The teacher must always keep in mind that his behavior toward a student will often be viewed by other students as a model of the kind of behavior they too should demonstrate toward that student. Consequently, when a teacher says to a student, "You are always giving me sloppy work" or "That was a dumb thing to do" or "You are always getting into trouble," many of the other students in the class may become inclined to form similar attitudes toward that student and perhaps eventually reject him and treat him with disgust. On the other hand, a student criticized by his classmates may eventually become accepted by them if the teacher treats him as a worthwhile and competent person. When a student like Billy offers a suggestion or makes a contribution, the teacher can communicate to the class that Billy has made a contribution by saying, for example, "That's an interesting way of looking at it, Billy."

As soon as Billy has completed a difficult task or solved a complicated problem, the teacher should express the excitement of success to both the student and his critical classmates. A simple, well-controlled "That's correct" or "Very good" will not be effective. The student has worked very hard to solve the problem, and the teacher must convey that what he has learned makes a difference and that somebody cares. The teacher should treat the student's accomplishment as the product of a monumental effort, which it was. Unless the teacher can show an honest appreciation of the student's effort, he may leave the student feeling "All that work for what? 'Very good.'" When the teacher can honestly express the excitement of success, he may say something like, "You've got it! I'm really proud of you, Billy. You see that, Greg? I told you he'd get it." The teacher who feels with the student and who uses the student's success to demonstrate that he is capable of learning is helping the student see himself as a competent problem-solver and a worthy person (37).

In many classroom activities the teacher can supplement his verbal statements about the student's progress and success by designing a visual progress record, such as a chart. The record would indicate to the student each of the activities, tasks, or problems he has completed. An accurate preparation of a visual progress record would require the teacher and student to come to an agreement each day concerning the particular activities the student has completed or the particular skills he has mastered and those activities and skill areas that he needs to work on further. Both the teacher and student need not only to establish standards to determine when work is satisfactorily completed, but also to determine *why* the student is successful in some things and unsuccessful in other things and how he can improve his performance. The student's self-confidence would be strengthened if detailed, positive written statements describing the specific competencies achieved supplemented the visual record. The student could use these statements to remind himself that he can succeed.

For inquiry-oriented learning programs, progress can be assessed effectively with summaries (92). A useful procedure is to summarize before and after each inquiry session the basic points made to date on the current issue. Summaries enable the group to check the meanings that have been communicated and determine whether or not there is a fairly accurate understanding of what has been said and settled. The teacher may say, "Before we go any further, let me see if I can restate what has been said." In his statements the teacher should reflect both the feelings and the ideas that have been expressed. The teacher would then ask the group to comment on the accuracy of his summary.

Summaries also enable each student to think critically about the issues—to examine simultaneously the evidence presented both for and against a point of view; to make progressively finer distinctions among words, meanings, and arguments; and to clarify, reconsider, or modify their previously expressed views. Finally, summaries help students separate the resolved issues from the unresolved ones, and this lessens the likelihood of rediscussing settled issues in future inquiry sessions. The teacher can communicate the progress made by listing the issues that have been resolved or temporarily set aside, and noting where there is agreement and disagreement in the group.

Simulations are perhaps most effectively analyzed and assessed through group discussions and the use of nonthreatening questions. Moreover, the actors in a simulation are less likely to feel threatened if they are asked to discuss the situation before the rest of the class engages in the analysis.

Questions posed to nonparticipants should be directed away from an analysis of the behavior of specific actors in the simulation. When the class feels that there is a climate of psychological safety and that there is acceptance of divergent ideas and feelings, more of the analysis may be directed toward the feelings of the actors, provided the teacher is aware of the possibility of mobilizing anxiety with which he may not wish to deal. An analysis of the actor's beliefs and motives in simulations involving racial prejudice or subjects of high emotional significance, such as sex taboos, may be quite traumatic for some students.

The analysis and teacher's questions should be designed to help students gather information on five items: (1) how the students feel about the simulation in general and the teacher's role in particular, (2) what new knowledge and skills each student feels he has acquired from the simulation, (3) how the simulation of real-world events could be improved and made more effective as a learning technique, (4) what new problems or new situations could be simulated, and (5) what new learning activities other than simulations would be appropriate to pursue at that time.

The teacher's role in assessing progress and in providing useful guidance can often be made more effective if each student writes out in his own words how he feels about the activity he has

just completed. A sentence-completion technique (fig. 5) may be a very effective tool for this purpose. The incomplete sentences can also be cast as oral questions.

A log book in which each student writes daily entries describing his fears, hopes, joys, and questions with regard to himself, his classmates, the teacher, and the subject is another effective means of securing his impressions about his progress and about the kind and amount of guidance he needs. The teacher can check the student's log each day to see whether some changes in classroom organization, the student's learning program, or the teacher's behavior are needed. The teacher, with the student's permission, may also want to record some of the log entries in his own copy of the student's learning folder to have a more complete record of the student's perceptions of classroom life.

Another technique for getting useful reactions from students and for helping them understand how and why they have progressed as they have, is for the teacher to conduct "How We Did" sessions at regular intervals. The teacher can ask students to share their feelings about how they succeeded, how they believe they came to learn all the things they learned, what strategies they believe are worth remembering for the future, and whether some of the problems or conflicts of the past disappeared through working as they have—by themselves or by working with others toward a common goal. For example, the teacher may ask: "What was it about your way of working that made this possible? Did your way of organizing yourselves have anything to do with it? What have you learned about ways of working that will help you with the next activity? Will this same process be helpful in out-of-school situations?" By questioning students on why things have worked out as they have, the teacher helps them recognize the individual growth they are achieving and why this growth is taking place; he helps them understand how their experience in past situations can be a guide in planning new experiences; and he helps them acquire the skill to make more appropriate choices and more effective decisions (93).

The teacher should also help his students examine different standards for selecting activities and projects, for forming groups,

Date_____
Your name_____
Subject_____
Teacher_____

Personal Reaction Form

In order to make the class more valuable to you, it would be helpful to know how you feel about what you have done. Your frank and thoughtful reactions to the activities we have just completed will be useful in planning and implementing learning programs for the future.

1. My overall reaction to the activity is that I ......

2. The things that I enjoyed learning about most were

3. The new things that I can do now are ....

4. The things that I have learned about myself are ...

5. The things I want to spend more time on are ......

6. The things that I don't care to do anymore are ....

7. I feel that working with others in the class is ....

8. If I could repeat the experience, I would ....

9. The class could be improved by ....

10. I would like it better if the teacher would ....

Figure 5.

and for evaluating progress, and help them determine whether or not some of the standards examined should be adopted by their class. Moreover, the teacher should help each student learn how to ask *himself* questions about the progress he is making, how to identify and establish valid standards of achievement, how to gather available evidence, and how to make judgments about the acceptability of his own work. This should not be interpreted to mean that ultimately the teacher will have no role in assessing the student's work. Assuredly, the teacher will always need to offer his own views about the student's performances. However, his appraisals are not imposed on the learner; rather, they are shared with him. The teacher says to the student, "Here are my observations about what you have set out to do, how you have tried to reach your goals, and how successful you have been in your efforts."

When the teacher and student share their observations about the direction and quality of classroom learning, the teacher may discover that the student's learning program needs to be modified. He may find that some of the activities are inappropriate, either because they are too easy or too difficult, or because they do not provide continuity and psychological relevance to the student's life. Also, as noted in Chapter 7, a student's concerns or goals may change markedly *before* a learning program is completed. For these reasons, a learning program must allow for modifications when necessary. Needless to say, the kind of change required depends on the new concerns and skills the student acquires or on the particular difficulties he is encountering in his efforts to complete his learning program. In some instances, the needed changes may be easily discovered. When they are not, the teacher and student will simply have to try out a number of different modifications to determine the particular learning goals, materials, activities, and kinds of help that are most appropriate for the student. Again, the student must find a balance between exploring his new concerns and fulfilling his agreement to complete an individual or group project. For some students, a time extension or a smaller number of tasks may be the most appropriate change. For others, a more suitable arrangement may be for them to undertake and complete two brief activities, perhaps simultaneously, rather than one long one. However, these students would not be free to undertake a third activity until they had completed one of their two planned acitvities. In short, the teacher has the responsibility of requiring the student to fulfill his basic commitments and of making the program modifications each student needs for success without having him develop a dislike for the activities he is completing.

Although I have described in detail how the teacher can establish an effective helping relationship with a student, it should be emphasized that not all help, or even the most useful help, always comes from the teacher. Many students learn more quickly and efficiently from their peers. Moreover, in view of the widespread concern about deteriorating interpersonal relations within families and between generations, races, and social classes, students must be given sufficient opportunities to learn to work more effectively with each other.

There are many advantages in having students help each other search for meaning and competence. A brighter student can often establish rapport and open communication with less bright students more effectively than adults can, as he is less likely to be regarded as an "authority figure." Also, a student is generally more willing to consider another student's suggestions for changing his behavior than those of an adult, because he perceives a greater opportunity for reciprocal influence. A slightly brighter student often provides a more realistic level of aspiration for a slower student than would an adult. Many students can accept correction about how they are trying to solve problems from other students more readily than they can from adults. Another advantage of the student-as-teacher approach is that the student who helps other students can test his own knowledge and skills, develop a realistic image of his own capabilities and present state of development, and come to an appreciation of those capabilities.

As suggested in Chapter 6, opportunities for students-as-teachers can be built into learning programs in the form of team learning or small group programs. Students can plan programs with each other, do their work and assess their progress together, and share whatever grades or results their joint effort yields, "just as adults must do in the real world" (76).

More and more teachers are recognizing that teaching and learning styles can be matched up in our classrooms not only by a teacher–student "fit" but also, and perhaps more easily, by a student–student fit. The student-as-teacher is clearly one of the most obvious ways in which a student can make a contribution to the school and to others while at the same time styling his own learning. When students are involved in the teaching process and can help other students, without being in competition with each other, the meaning and usefulness of education is seen more clearly. The teacher will continue to be very important to students, but for a different reason—he will be needed as a resource to help students work with each other. When the teacher views each student as having valuable ideas and skills to share with others and as being able to help others build new mental models and acquire more skills, he sees his role as one of facilitating the sharing and building process.

Up to this point I have described how a student can learn from others. However, since an avowed goal of American public education is to help our young people style their own learning and determine for themselves the direction and quality of their education, the teacher will need to help each student assume increasing amounts of responsibility in planning and implementing his own learning programs. Because of the tradition in our schools of keeping students dependent on teachers, the stage of self-directed learning usually can be achieved only after a transitional process —i.e., only after learners have moved through several phases in which they exercise increasing amounts of control over the design and implementation of each aspect of their learning programs.

There is no single set of procedures that should be followed or that is effective in helping each learner take on the increased responsibilities of directing his own learning. This is because learning programs can vary in kind and level and because students differ markedly in the rates at which they can assume responsibility. These facts alone suggest that the teacher will need to try out a variety of techniques to determine which are the most effective for helping each student move toward the total management of his own learning. Nevertheless, some suggestions can be offered to help teachers undertake the transition from joint determination of learning programs to student-managed learning programs.

It may be more practical if at first the transition is limited to the planning phase of learning programs. This approach keeps manageable the number of items over which the learner will need to assume control at one time. After the student can assume complete control over program planning, transitions in other aspects of the management process can be undertaken.

To complete a satisfactory transition in the area of program planning, five steps may be employed to grant the student a larger role than the teacher in the five program components of (1) selecting the kinds of learning activities to be completed, (2) planning and organizing the materials, equipment, and resources needed to undertake the learning activities, (3) devising a schedule for completing each activity, (4) determining the grade to be received when each activity is completed, and (5) establishing a deadline for modifying a learning contract. In step one, the student may exercise increased responsibility by assuming complete control over any *one* of these five program components, while sharing joint control over the remaining four components. In step two, the student would assume complete control over any *two* program planning components and share joint control over the remaining three components. This procedure would continue through step five, at which point the student would assume complete control of all five aspects of program planning.

When the student is able to demonstrate that he can assume full control of program planning and discharge this responsibility effectively, the teacher can help him assume increasing amounts of responsibility for each of the following: (1) determining how he can gather reliable information about the way he is learning and about how he can best find the answers and solutions he is seeking, (2) keeping his own record of his progress, which the teacher can review periodically, (3) determining when his learning program needs to be modified and how the changes should be made, and (4) determining when he has completed his entire learning program satisfactorily and can plan and organize a new learning program.

In effect, the teacher needs to help the student acquire the skills to determine for himself how well he is doing, where and why he is correct, where and why he is in error, what he needs to do to improve his performance, and how to keep a detailed progress and self-guidance chart itemizing each of the activities completed and each of the activities and activity segments he still needs to complete. For example, the student needs to learn how to correct his own spelling, how to proofread his own written work, how to check his own math problems, and how to keep a log and construct a checklist. The teacher also needs to help the student learn how to select samples of his work for reference and comparison a week or a month later, since in this way he would have at hand concrete evidence of his own development. Perhaps the teacher can use individual conferences with each student as a way to set this process in motion.

To summarize: the teacher's basic responsibility in building a helping relationship with students, individually and in groups, is to have students continually examine and recognize the specific ways they are conducting their search for meaning and competence. The help the teacher gives may be as little as posing an occasional thought-provoking question or as much as breaking down a task into small steps, asking and parlaying a variety of questions, and arranging frequent individual conferences. The student's current skills, his rate and style of learning, and his feelings about his progress are the teacher's most reliable guides for determining the kind and amount of help to give—for designing questions, for arranging materials and tasks sequentially, and for delegating the kind and amount of responsibility each student needs to direct his own learning.

9

Some Questions and Doubts

PREDICTABLY, whenever a teacher is offered suggestions for modifying his classroom in ways that help each student direct his own learning, he counters with questions about how to handle some of the time-honored teaching practices, e.g., grades and discipline, and he expresses doubts about the feasibility of implementing the suggestions. Although I cannot anticipate all the questions a teacher may raise about designing and operating a shared classroom, I would like to discuss some of the more important concerns he may have.

"How Do I Meet Thirty-five Different Students' Needs?"

It has been pointed out that since no single set of learning conditions can help *all* students develop optimally, the teacher must discover and provide the different conditions that different students need to succeed in their learning efforts. However, the fact that each student needs particular learning conditions to do his best learning does not mean that if the teacher has thirty-five students he must provide thirty-five different sets of activities and thirty-five different kinds of help at the same time in his classroom. In a shared classroom, *appropriate* learning conditions are not necessarily *separate* learning conditions for each student. Admittedly, at times it will be appropriate for students to work independently on their own activities, but at other times it will be appropriate for them to work in pairs, in small groups, or as a total class to achieve common goals and solve common problems.

Moreover, in a shared classroom the teacher is not the only person who facilitates learning or meets the needs of students. As we have discussed in Chapter 8, learning and teaching are measurably improved when students teach one another. This approach is feasible in almost every classroom, simply because individual differences in knowledge, skills, and learning rates always produce some students who have a greater understanding of an issue or problem or who are nearer to the point of complete mastery of a skill than other students.

The teacher who operates a shared classroom will find that when students are involved in planning, directing, and evaluating their own learning and especially when they help each other, he can easily triple the time and attention he would otherwise have for each student. Students can also help with the record-keeping and clerical tasks. Some mothers and fathers in the community on occasion will give some of their time. For example, a father who devotes one hour each week or so to a group of students and shares his valuable experience or craft skills will not only be able to help out with the teaching, but he will make learning more reality-oriented, he will learn to grow along with his youngsters, and he will learn more realistically how schools operate and how much they need various kinds of community support.

Further, meeting students' needs in a shared classroom does not necessarily mean that the teacher must be busily trying to have each of his thirty-five students achieve complete mastery of the same skill or of different skills. Since no two students begin a learning event with the same knowledge and capabilities, and since no two students progress at the same rate in acquiring a particular skill, it is unrealistic to expect all students to achieve complete mastery or the same level of progress in a given area, especially since all students are learning within the same fixed period of time. Clearly, just as the teacher must suspend his expectations about what his students should be able to do when they enter his classroom, so too must he suspend his expectations of what they should be able to do when they leave his classroom.

When a teacher considers the brief time for which he has his students, the different skill levels they display upon entering his classroom, and the different rates of progress they display during the time they share together, the most he can hope is that each student will make some significant progress in mastering something (and the student *should* master something if the teacher arranges appropriate learning conditions). Some students, because of their high entry levels and fast rates of learning, will achieve complete mastery of many skills, including that of managing their own learning. However, for students with lower entry levels and slower rates of learning, significant progress may be partial mastery of a few skills or complete mastery of one skill, or significant improvement in the ability to share responsibility for planning and implementing a learning program, to keep commitments, or to share materials and equipment with others. The teacher must recognize that, if each student is to develop according to his own sense of himself, he must be permitted to acquire his own skills in his own way and in his own time. Further, the teacher must recognize that when each student fulfills his commitments completely, his accomplishments must be valued as highly as the accomplishments of the fastest and most productive learner in the classroom, regardless of how his new skill levels compare with those of other students in the class. The teacher can help each of his thirty-five students become competent not by having them compete with each other and establish winners or losers or by trying to have each of them achieve complete mastery of the same skill or even of different skills within the same period of time, but by helping each student attain a significant degree of achievement in an area in which he had little knowledge or competence before he began his learning program (92).

Unlike many elementary teachers who have one group of students and can spend several hours each day getting to know where each of his students is and where he wants to go, the teacher in a departmentalized high school may have five or six groups of students whom he meets for only one hour a day. Can such a teacher deal competently with the individual needs of each of his 150 or 200 students? I believe he can, because the amount of available time for each student is not so important as the manner in which the available time is used. The single most important ingredient in successfully conducting a shared classroom is the way the teacher capitalizes on his single greatest resource for teaching—the students themselves. It is the teacher's skill in helping students help themselves that is critical. The teacher who can help his students help each other—to find out where they are, establish their own goals, plan their own activities, and teach each other to achieve their goals—can meet the needs of each of his students whether he has one group of thirty-five or five groups of thirty-five students each. The converse is also true: the teacher who does not organize his classroom so that students can help each other learn will have a difficult time meeting each student's needs even if he has only fifteen students a day. It is not the amount of time or the number of students the teacher has that is decisive in conducting a shared classroom; it is the extent to which the teacher views classroom life as a shared experience and helps each student share his skills with others.

Thus, although each student is at a different starting point in his search for meaning and competence and will display a different rate and style of learning in conducting his search and achieving his goal, the teacher can make use of many techniques and resources to arrange appropriate learning conditions for each student. He can have faster learners help students who are learning at a slower rate; he can provide all students with a wide range of activities designed to facilitate discovery either on the same problem, issue, question, or task, or on different ones; he can help some students work independently, and others to work in pairs and in small groups teaching each other; and he can establish as a standard of satisfactory achievement for each student a degree of progress that represents significant achievement for *him*. The teacher must recognize that, in a shared classroom, students' learning patterns are his best single guide for discovering and employing appropriate teaching strategies, and that the students themselves are his best single resource for arranging appropriate learning conditions. If the teacher will let him, each student can help the teacher be successful. With the teacher's help, each student in each classroom can find out where he is in his knowledge and skills and can plan and complete appropriate learning programs. The classroom belongs to both teacher and student, and together they can learn to arrive at decisions and employ practices that help each other achieve new levels of competence and maturity.

"Should a Student Ever Fail?"

This question is best answered by examining the purpose and nature of evaluation. Evaluation should not be a process that takes place after and apart from learning, which produces a surprise or disappointment for the student and over which the student has no control. Evaluation should be an integral part of the learning process, conducted for the purpose of helping the student improve on his past performance.

The teacher needs to gather and interpret information about a student's current concerns and skills *before, during,* and *after* the student plans and implements his learning program, in order to make accurate judgments about the most appropriate help he can give the student. Consequently, evaluation is not distinguished from the helping relationship, but provides the basis for giving help. A grade, therefore, reflects the appropriateness of the teacher's helping techniques and the extent to which the student has fulfilled his program commitments.

A clear implication of this approach is that no student should be allowed to reach the point where he receives a grade that reflects failure. In fact, if the learning activities selected and the help provided are appropriate, it is impossible for a student to receive a grade of Unsatisfactory or F. If a learning program did not enable a student to achieve a level of competency acceptable to both the teacher and himself—i.e., the student made an unacceptable number of errors or he was unable to complete a planned activity, or both—the learning program should have been modified or restructured so that he was able to achieve some mastery of skills. When the teacher helps the student in the manner and at the time he needs it, the student should not only succeed at something, but he should be able to see the kind of grade he is earning —a grade that indicates progress and some degree of mastery. He may not have mastered what other students mastered, but he should have become competent in some important area of the subject. The grade he receives should confirm the fact that he mastered valuable skills.

The preceding point and the discussion on the previous question suggest that grades need to distinguish and represent accurately the *degrees* of mastery that students achieve in their activities. Many students may demonstrate only partial mastery after a specified period of time, while others may achieve greater degrees of mastery. Consequently, since each student should be provided with the help he needs to succeed at something and should be graded in terms of the degree of mastery he achieves, an A, B, C, or Incomplete grading system can be defended. Under such a system, the student could convert an Incomplete to a C by achieving minimum acceptable mastery in an area, and a student could convert a grade of B or C to an A by achieving greater mastery if he wished to do so.

A teacher may be prompted to ask, "Would a bright student who has done relatively little to add to his already superior knowledge in a subject receive an Incomplete, while a less able student still struggling with basic skills receive an A for having worked hard and having mastered only a few of these skills?" It is to be hoped that the teacher would not let the bright student do "relatively little." Although a student may have a superior level of knowledge and competency in a subject, there are always new areas and levels that he can investigate. There are always additional reality-oriented activities that the student can design and engage in on his own or with others, and there are always competencies that he can help other students acquire, thereby improving and refining his own competencies.

A teacher may also ask, "Isn't it misleading and unfair to give two students the same A for making substantial progress beyond their starting points when the first student can learn faster and demonstrate more skills in a subject than the second student?" The answer is no, *if* the system of reporting progress and achievement does each of the following: (*1*) lists each of the skills the student attempted to master in each subject (e.g., in second-grade arithmetic the list would include skills in addition, subtraction, measurement, graph-reading, et cetera); (*2*) indicates the level of mastery the student did achieve in each skill; and (*3*) indicates the time the student took to achieve his level of mastery in each skill. When a student may take whatever time he needs to master a skill and when a reporting system provides detailed and comprehensive information about the student's level of mastery and learning rate in each skill area of each subject explored, students with very different learning rates can receive superior grades for their achievements.

Two other points are important to note before leaving the question of failing a student. First, when a student does not complete the requirements of a program that he has *not* selected and helped to plan, it would be grossly unfair for the teacher to pass judgment on the acceptability of the student's work. In the absence of freedom to participate in planning a learning program, no commitment can be expected or required of the student; and, in the absence of freedom to choose, no responsibility or accountability can be assigned to him.

Second, when a student chooses not to complete a program that he and his teacher jointly discussed, planned, and agreed on, the student still should not be viewed as a failure, nor should he be assigned a grade labeling him one. Despite the fact that he chooses not to complete his work, the grade F provides no more encouragement or help to succeed than an Incomplete. Only, an Incomplete says to the student, "if you want to receive a grade signifying satisfactory progress, you need to do more work."

Clearly, if education is to be truly open-ended, if each student is to be able to improve on his present skills, then the grading system must encourage continuous self-improvement. Whenever a student receives less than an A for his work, he should have the option of completing the additional work needed to receive an

A. A grading system that facilitates learning places no restrictions on the level of competency a student may want to achieve and on the amount of time he needs to achieve it. Consequently, a grading system that includes the grade F cannot be defended. The grade F and the label "failure" do not facilitate self-improvement. They always prevent it from taking place and they often destroy the very individuals who most desperately need satisfying educational experience. If our schools are to be successful in helping our youth develop the best that is in them, they must eliminate the grade F and the punitive and slanderous label "failure" (92).

"How Do I Group?"

We have stated that since each student learns in his own way and from the framework of his own present understandings, he must have a significant role in determining his methods of learning. We have also emphasized that it is a *shared* classroom, with each student having autonomy which is circumscribed by the rights of others. In this context, then, how does grouping occur?

The composition of a group should be a natural one, comprised not of students similar in IQ or achievement-test scores, but of students who at a given time have common concerns and purposes. Although a group activity may be suggested by one or more students, it should always be initiated through the interaction of teacher and students. I believe the teacher must be involved in a grouping process because of the negative feelings and attitudes some students may have toward other students and because of their tendency to exclude those whom they fear or dislike. The teacher is simply exercising his right to see that each student's rights are protected and that a shared environment takes in unpopular members. The teacher also recognizes that the group experience is an important opportunity for helping students break down some of the interpersonal fears and dislikes they bring to the classroom.

In the group activity, each student has a part and responsibility in deciding his form of participation, although the group as a whole will have specific goals. The teacher must require students within each group to reach agreement on the group's purpose and to specify the particular contribution each member will make toward achieving that purpose. Each individual in the group must make a commitment to achieving the group's goals and must be accountable to the group for his contribution. Again, the teacher has the responsibility to monitor the group's behavior, especially since peers are inclined to be more harsh with a student who may want to break a commitment than the teacher would be.

Often several learning groups may be organized to conduct different activities simultaneously. The teacher's role in working with several groups is a dynamic one. He moves from one group to another, engaging in a variety of direct encounters with students. He may listen to one group of students read or debate, help a second group plan a simulation, and observe a third group design a map. He is continually asking students questions to augment his awareness of how much they understand of what they are doing and where they are going, and to determine how he can help them succeed.

In a shared classroom, regardless of whether the students in each group work on similar projects or on different tasks, they would discuss with each other the work at hand. In fact, since teachers know that students learn from one another and since a fundamental purpose of the educational process is to help each individual acquire the skills to communicate effectively with others, the teacher would encourage students to arrange desks and tables in ways that help them conduct worthwhile discussions. Also, he would lead discussions to help students discover how they can provide each other with constructive criticism. Each group member would learn how he could find help from the other members of the group if he needed it. For example, if one student is reading slowly or is having difficulty with his math, he could get help from a friend and would not need to approach the teacher for assistance every time he had a problem. The teacher would aim to create a sense of family within each group.

"Will Students Be Honest?"

When it comes to designing and operating a classroom that gives increasing responsibility to the student to manage his own learning, most teachers are inclined to believe that students cannot be trusted, that they will cheat more often on a self-directed learning program than on a teacher-managed program.

There will be little or no cheating under a student-centered learning system in which decision-making is shared, because in a shared classroom the conditions needed to ensure successful learning and to prevent cheating have been arranged. In such a classroom, each student (1) selects and organizes learning activities he wants to and can complete, (2) receives the kind and amount of help he needs, (3) earns and receives the grade he chose to work for, and (4) increasingly develops a view of himself as a competent and worthy person. In these conditions a student will not be dishonest; he will not cheat himself out of something he *wants* to do or receive or become.

It is important to note that, although most teachers who are concerned about cheating are also quite sincere in wanting to improve the way they operate their classrooms, some have no intention of taking the steps to acquire the skills and self-confidence they themselves need to design a more democratic and productive classroom. These teachers cover up their fears of change by criticizing any new method that would make significant demands on them. Sometimes they say, "It doesn't work, I've already tried it." Perhaps some did try a version of a new teaching approach but were so misguided in their experiment and/or bungled it so badly and felt so humiliated that they refused to allow themselves to try out another new approach. Consequently teachers need to ask themselves, "Am I skeptical about using a new classroom approach because I believe it isn't realistic or workable, or because I am unsure of myself or afraid that I and my students may find out that I cannot operate a classroom unless I am a dictator?"

"Will Students Become Well-educated?"

The teacher may also be prompted to ask, "If teachers arrange learning conditions so that the learning activities that comprise the curriculum are jointly determined by students and teacher, can we be sure that each student will master the basic school subjects—reading, writing, and arithmetic—and that he will pursue high standards of achievement in areas such as physics and foreign languages?" I believe the answer is an unequivocal yes. When we systematically examine shared classrooms, we find that students can acquire acceptable levels of competency in communication skills and in any subject they investigate. Students do not need to be pressed into particular kinds of learning activities to develop into socially competent individuals. The key, of course, rests with the kinds of learning conditions the teacher provides. If students are provided with either too little or too much direction in planning and conducting their activities, or if they find that the conditions of learning are demeaning and senseless, they will avoid commitment and will not achieve the levels of competency they need to communicate effectively and to solve personal and social problems. If, on the other hand, students find the conditions of learning relevant, nonthreatening, and supportive, and if they are exposed to a variety of problems and interpersonal situations that necessitate the acquisition and use of important skills, they will learn everything they need to learn. It is interesting to note that, under the present educational system, mastery of the three R's and many other subjects is achieved by only about half of our students. I believe that under an effective system of shared management all students will acquire all the skills they need to be well-educated, competent, and productive members of society.

"How Is 'Discipline' Established
in a Shared Classroom?"

Without question, cooperation is needed in any social context if individual or group goals are to be achieved. However, cooperation (which is a term I prefer to "discipline") does not occur in a vacuum, nor can it be pursued as an end in itself. The conditions that each student needs in order to learn—trust, support, freedom, commitment, and guidance—are also the conditions that facilitate the development of constructive interpersonal behavior patterns. Consequently, if a student's learning program does not take into account his concerns and skills, does not require him to keep agreed-upon commitments, and does not provide the emotional support and help he needs, he will most certainly search for something that *does* provide him with some sense of accomplishment—and that "something" may include acting out his dissatisfaction with the learning program. If, on the other hand, the student finds that his learning program is meeting his needs, and if he feels that he is developing worthwhile skills by continuing with his learning program, few interpersonal problems will develop.

Further, as noted earlier, each student has certain psychological needs—for self-importance, competence, acceptance, and power—which are arranged in terms of priorities. The teacher must help each student meet his most urgent needs constructively. Otherwise, the student will search for his own ways of meeting them. Classroom behavior is always an expression of how a student feels about himself and the way his needs are being met. The hostile, aggressive student who dominates or bullies another student may be expressing his need to feel important. However, the classroom as it is presently organized may not permit him to develop a feeling of self-importance and competence. Perhaps the student who clowns and disrupts the class is saying, "I want to be noticed and appreciated, and I am not finding this here." Perhaps the student who will not commit himself to or complete an activity is saying, "I want to do something that *I* think is important."

It is also important to remember that each student has a need to express his feelings to others. A group of adults working out a problem need to talk to each other about their feelings; students have the same need. However, when no opportunities are made available for students to satisfy this need or when efforts to satisfy it are thwarted, feelings get bottled up and may explode into physical attacks. Our knowledge of human behavior tells us that "children who can express their anger safely without fear of reprimand or punishment, and then proceed to examine the sources of their anger, are far less likely to hit each other" (38).

Problems of "discipline" also arise when students are not permitted to search for answers to the most meaningful problems in their own lives—e.g., war, racial conflicts, family strife, and alienation. Yet so many schools avoid these subjects entirely or make their consideration a meaningless sequence of tasks and exercises that each student must struggle to complete. Schools, by ignoring the critical issues that students are involved in here and now, are unwittingly creating their own discipline problems. When the bell rings, schools demand that students suspend their lives, pretend that their concerns and problems do not exist, take their seats, and open their books. No wonder students are inattentive, restless, and "unmotivated." No wonder they become "discipline" problems (38).

In most classrooms, rules and routines are established to avoid controversy and disagreements. Controversy and conflict are not permitted to be a part of group life because teachers do not see their responsibility of helping each person share his hopes, fears, values, and competencies in a real way. However, in a shared classroom there is openness, honesty, and a sense of family. There is considerable give-and-take, disagreement, and even argument, because these are characteristics inherent in the life of an open group.

Teachers must also recognize that when people do things together in organized face-to-face situations, whether the period of time is a year, a day, or an hour, problems will arise regardless of the nature of the group or the environment in which they work. It is sometimes forgotten that each classroom is comprised of a variety of interactions occurring simultaneously between several individuals, each of whom differs in his concerns, competencies, and energy levels, and each of whom is changing in each of these characteristics depending on the hour of day, the activity being undertaken, and the availability of materials and help.

Consequently, the teacher should expect youngsters at times to have arguments and even fights. These interpersonal conflicts occur naturally when two or more people must share the same environment, and they should be viewed as learning opportunities for both the teacher and student. Teachers must learn to look upon classroom problems not as deterrents to learning but as opportunities to improve individual and group problem-solving skills.

When conflicts do arise, the teacher should refrain from assigning blame and instead try to focus on integrating the group and improving learning conditions for the individual students who may be having difficulties. Let us look at how one teacher handled a very minor classroom incident in this way.

In a second-grade classroom, students were busy working on their own arithmetic activities. While the teacher was moving about the room, helping each child as he needed it, Anthony lost interest in his planned activity and got up from his desk and wandered over to the science table. He became interested in watching Pogo, the class rabbit.

Within seconds, Anthony had opened the door to Pogo's cage, and the rabbit leaped out and began hopping around the room. Predictably, the children laughed, squealed, and moved about in their seats to get a better view of the "science happening." The teacher remained calm, recognizing that nothing would be gained by scolding the children for being themselves or by criticizing Anthony for pursuing his new interest. She decided that the first thing to do was to get Pogo back in the cage.

She asked the students to help her corner Pogo while she edged over to grasp the rabbit. After she returned him to his cage, she remarked, "I'll put Pogo up on a higher shelf where he might

not jump as easily while we go on with our planned activities."
Then she walked casually about the room, at first asking the students whether any of them had already finished their activities, then stopping to share her observations with one child about his progress and asking another whether he was having any difficulty with his activity or whether he would like to talk about his progress with her. Although Anthony did not-request her help, she did go over to Anthony minutes later and ask him how he was progressing. She then talked with him about the rabbit incident and discovered that he was, in fact, bored with his activity. Anthony and the teacher then reappraised the planned activity and arrived at a decision about what Anthony could work on for the remainder of the period.

The teacher viewed this incident as a natural problem occurring in group living; she was composed; she moved to where the trouble was; she didn't make a public issue of the incident, and she didn't blame. She relied on the students to help restore the group's positive interactions, and she quickly eased the students back into the planned activities. She found a casual way to talk with Anthony to find out how he was progressing and to make some new decisions about the remainder of his learning program.

To be sure, in other situations the teacher may have to take a different tack—for example, with students who have learned to deal with conflicts in ways very different from and less constructive than those the teacher uses. In *The Culturally Deprived Child* (131), Frank Riessman reports how a teacher in a ghetto school had to be quite firm to develop cooperation without coercing her students or turning them into sheep or slaves. While the specific, concrete advice she offers is for teaching in the elementary school, I believe her ideas are equally applicable to dealing with older students.

> Miss L. told us she starts her first class with a full question-and-answer discussion of what she calls the ground rules of the course. She begins:
> "You and I are going to live together for the next year. . . . Now, to do this we need some rules." She then asks them to discuss why certain rules, such as "no running in class," are necessary.

During the hour some child will usually raise his hand and ask whether he can get a drink of water. In response she says, "You're too old to *ask* for water; *tell me* you want a drink and unless I need you here that very minute it will be OK with me if you go."

Another thing that happens every opening day is the "initiation" of the teacher. "This is a highly organized, cooperative effort to break the new teacher. They want to see how smart you are, how much you can stand. So one child says it's too light in the room—can we pull down the shades. Then another one complains it's too dark—can we pull them up. Somebody else is too warm and wants the windows open, while still another party is too cold. This is a game the kids love to play."

And what is the teacher supposed to do, we asked? "Stand firm, show that you're wise to the game, kid about it, but don't go along with it. You are the master of the ship and you will decide when it's too cold, too light, and so on. . . ."

After about three weeks the class has a period of mutual evaluation in which they discuss how well the teacher has been living up to her part of the bargain, and vice versa. Some child may tell her that she hasn't paid enough attention to some other child. When the criticisms are accurate, "and they often are," she accepts them and tries to correct the situation. The children learn soon enough that they can depend on her, that she will stand by what she says. For example, one day the teacher stated that a news story appearing in the *New York Daily News* was also in the *New York Times.* The children said it wasn't. Miss L. replied that she would eat the newspaper if it wasn't in the *Times,* because she was so dead sure she was right. The following day she discovered that she had been wrong, whereupon she obtained a cake from the school cafeteria, stuffed the newspaper inside of it, and ate it in front of the entire class. . . .

"Another thing about discipline—when I apply the rules, I never get indignant and I don't humiliate the child. The rules are purely objective and I'm only 'sorry' that they have violated them and therefore require punishment. I get the children to realize that all of us have to accept the consequences of our behavior. And I repeat over and over again that breaking the rules means 'I can't teach you. I can only think that you do not want to learn.' Of course, punishment and threats should be rare—you shouldn't have to punish children often. It's more of a last resort and loses its meaning if it becomes habitual. For most common occurrences, I am more prone to say to the disobeying child, 'You are letting me down—you're breaking our agreement.' One thing is certain, these kids want limits. It's time we get over the idea that discipline means rigidity and dictatorship. The deprived child thrives on rules and order and if he respects and likes you, he hasn't the least desire to rebel. He wants you to be firm, but responsive. Firmness doesn't mean brutality or hardness. To brutality he responds in kind, and then the classroom becomes a jungle. . . ."

We then queried Miss L. on what she did when the children used vile language.

"Mainly roll with the punches, never get flabbergasted, show that you know the lingo, and are not 'stuck up.' Answer or deal with whatever they have said irrespective of the language, and then, as sort of an afterthought, remark that 'we do not use that kind of language in this class, please.' And don't think I haven't gotten unrequested apologies, sometimes as much as a week later."

How about fighting—what do you do about that, we asked? "I make it perfectly clear that I have nothing against fighting, that it's OK to know how to defend yourself, but in my classroom I can't teach you if there are going to be fisticuffs. If a fight is already in progress, I very often ask the two or three biggest boys in the class to help break it up—if they are not already involved in it, that is. Or sometimes I tap one of the combatants on the shoulder and ask if he has a match." [Pp. 89–93]

Miss L. is firm but not harsh. Students have a say and she listens to what they have to say. Yet, she utilizes the constructive behavior she must to deal with the behavior patterns the students display. She implies that while there is no single way of managing a cooperative class, there is no excuse for being destructive. Physical abuse by a teacher does not deal with the causes of interpersonal conflicts. On the contrary, hostility toward the teacher may develop to compound the hostility the fighting students have toward each other. The teacher must find out why the conflict or fighting developed and ask the involved students to help him find a satisfactory solution to the problem.

It is appropriate to point out again the importance for teachers of listening empathically when helping students resolve conflicts. As noted earlier, empathic, nonjudgmental listening is an essential first step in having an individual feel safe enough in a situation to look at his own behavior. Empathic listening is a caring type of listening—listening that says, "I understand how you feel and what you are saying." It is a listening that decodes the student's words to find the real meaning he is communicating. For example, when an empathic listener hears the angry student say, "You're a son of a bitch," he can decode it and respond, "Gee, you are really angry with me." This form of listening helps the student begin to examine what other feelings he may have, what these feelings mean to him, where he sees his feelings leading him, and what he might be able to do to deal competently with them.

When a student's behavior or language disrupts a planned activity, the teacher is strongly tempted to respond with judgmental statements. Judgmental statements are "you are" statements— "You're a loudmouth" or "You're a troublemaker." "You are" statements ascribe motives to a person's behavior and appraise his worth as a person. Consequently, the teacher who responds with "You are" statements to a student's unacceptable behavior may provoke hostility and escalate the conflict.

An honest and constructive response that a teacher can make when a student disrupts a planned activity is an "I feel" statement —"I'm feeling very angry about this loud noise." The teacher describes how he feels rather than what he thinks about someone else, because he has no reliable information about the true motives for another person's behavior.

The next step in trying to resolve conflicts in the classroom is for the teacher to avoid the use of a win–lose method—a method by which one person (who is almost always the teacher) gets his way and the other does not. The win–lose method, which was noted briefly in Chapter 7, is a power struggle in which each person has his own solution to the conflict and is trying to persuade or force the other person to accept it. Each person has the attitude "I want my way and I'm going to fight to get it" (64). Each person is unconcerned about the needs of the other. When a solution is reached, one person goes away feeling angry, defeated, and, frequently, hostile toward the person who defeated him. The teacher–student relationship in many of our schools today is often a power struggle, because the win–lose method is the only one used.

The alternative to the win–lose method is conflict-resolution by mutual agreement, which is quite commonly utilized in our society in families and labor–management disputes and which is the basic principle involved in planning and conducting learning programs in a shared classroom. The teacher asks the student to participate with him in a joint search for some solution that would be acceptable to both. One or both offer possible solutions, which are critically evaluated until eventually they decide on one that is acceptable to both. There is no need to persuade the other person to accept a solution, because each person shares in the decision-making and no one loses. No power is required to force compliance, because no one resists the decision. Predictably, since students rebel not against teachers but against teachers' arbitrary use of power, and since no power is used, there will be no hostility, resentment, or rebellion (64).

A final point that grows out of the preceding discussion on conflict-resolution is that students will recognize the necessity for reasonable school policies, and they will face and intelligently solve individual and group problems if they are given a significant voice in governing their own behavior. As was noted earlier, people are more likely to accept and adhere to behavioral standards when they take part in formulating and enforcing the rules and regulations than when the standards or rules are made up and enforced by others. Consequently, in the shared classroom, students, with the teacher's help, set up their own rules for classroom behavior and they decide on how the rules will be observed. It is perhaps desirable at the beginning of the year if the teacher and students together formulate a class code and place it on a chart at the front of the classroom. They may revise the code at the beginning of each term or marking period if they wish.

A steering and grievance committee may also be advantageous in establishing rules and facilitating conflict-resolution in a class. The class could elect 20 per cent of its members to the committee, which would meet periodically with the teacher to establish a set of class rules and to reevaiuate them and establish new ones when necessary. The committee would also recommend courses of action when rules are broken. A majority vote by the class would be needed before a rule would be considered binding or before a course of action could be taken. The teacher, however, would have the authority to veto a rule or course of action whenever he felt that the rights of some students would not be adequately protected. New elections would be held every six weeks or at the end of each grading period or school term in order to rotate membership on the committee.

Often things do not go smoothly during the formation and operation of steering and grievance committees. Arguments, apathy and resistance frequently occur, especially at the beginning, and must be taken in stride. Difficulties are experienced in almost every growth process. However, the maturity that students gain from their labor far outweighs the problems they might encounter. When the teacher permits his students to participate in the formation of rules and in the arbitration of conflicts, they are learning in the only reliable way they can how to govern themselves.

Unfortunately, too few teachers permit students to learn how to govern themselves. Even some of the teachers who claim to be democratic in operating their classrooms unintentionally manipulate their students. They believe that their duty as teachers is not to have students formulate and apply their own ideas about the most desirable conduct for specific situations, but to require students to establish rules of "good" behavior as the teachers conceive them. Inevitably, such teachers evoke resistance in students, because students eventually perceive the process of establishing "their own" standards as no more than a request to restate the behavior already established and enforced by the school (86).

However, an inexperienced student, with immature judgment and values, should not be expected to make all the major decisions about his interpersonal conduct and to style all of his behavior without help. Such an expectation is not only unrealistic but may also be terribly threatening to a student. Learning to use one's own behavior in constructive ways and to work productively with others is a developmental process. Each student must be given sufficient time and practice to learn self-direction, with a corresponding release from restraints. Increased responsibility of self-direction should be placed on a student at a pace that he can handle and to the extent that he can understand the consequences of his acts and can avoid trespassing on the freedom of others. Granted, students must be the instruments of their own development, and they need to develop the skills to behave cooperatively. However, freedom and responsibility are always defined in terms of the individual student's level of awareness and skills.

We have considered some of the major questions that the teacher may have about operating a shared classroom—questions about the applicability of the new methods; the procedures for dealing with time-honored practices such as grading, individualizing, and "discipline"; the extent to which students can be trusted to learn what they need to learn; and the extent to which the teacher has the skills to make the more desirable teaching techniques work effectively in his classroom. There *are* satisfactory answers to the teacher's questions, and, more importantly, the teacher *can* successfully make the transition to the shared classroom.

10

Making the Transition

THERE IS ALWAYS a gap between believing in the shared classroom and having the skills to design and operate one. For the teacher who is trying to wean himself away from a benevolent dictatorship, the task is indeed formidable. As is the case when learning any set of complex skills, the development of effective teaching practices evolves out of a series of experiments—of conceptualizing and trying out various strategies. To avoid being faced with highly stressful situations, the teacher bent on change must implement his new strategies in parts—he must try out one part of his strategy at a time and add a new part only when he feels he has mastered the previous one.

Where a given teacher might begin to initiate changes that facilitate self-directed learning in his students is hard to say. Each teacher has to decide on ways and begin in areas that make sense to him. At the elementary level, a teacher might start by making self-selection of reading materials possible in a reading group and gradually allow this procedure to spread to other areas of the curriculum.

Another teacher may try to help each student identify his current skills by means of an informal diagnostic test and then help him select something appropriate for his level. For example, the teacher could listen to a student read, and if the student misses more than 10 per cent of the words on a page, the teacher would ask the student to read from less difficult material. If the student misses few or no words, the teacher would give him books at higher levels until he could discover the level of difficulty at which he needs or wants reading instruction. In arithmetic, the teacher could present the student with various reality-oriented problems requiring addition, subtraction, et cetera, to discover what he understands well and what he wants to and can do. Thus, by checking what the student already knows and where he has problems, the teacher doesn't waste his or the student's time by having him work on something irrelevant to his skills and rate and style of learning.

The teacher can also begin to move toward a shared classroom by starting with students' common out-of-class experiences and then exploring the different directions the experiences could take. The students can be assisted in planning and conducting various kinds of inquiry sessions and skill-developing activities simultaneously. A high school biology teacher could start with a question to which all the students are able to respond in some way: "Who had breakfast this morning?" The question could lead to a discussion of digestion or hunger or nutrition or dental care. As a consequence, some students may want to trace the changes that take place in a piece of food during the digestive process, while others may want to use mechanical and chemical processes to simulate the digestion of particular kinds of food. A third group may be interested in the problem of hunger and may wish to interview local antipoverty officials and civil rights leaders to gather facts and obtain different perspectives on hunger in the community; and a fourth group may be interested in relationships between hunger, disease, poverty, ignorance, and frustration. An official from a local hospital may be willing to share with students some medical data and case histories that would help the students examine their concerns and study the problems more fully. Perhaps each group of students will find that their study crosses over into other subjects, and through the help of the biology teacher and other teachers they may be able to carry out interdisciplinary investigations, e.g., "How can we best fight hunger?" or "How can we help the disadvantaged rise from the bottom of the socio-economic ladder?" (38).

When the teacher breaks down the boundaries between traditionally separate subjects and puts away predesigned sequences of topics, and instead encourages students to ask their own questions about the world around them, he is not only encouraging individuality and the pursuit of self-directed learning but is providing students with opportunities to explore areas of study and utilize approaches to knowledge that have historically been kept out of the classroom by the constraints of curriculum guides.

The teacher at the elementary level might start making changes by utilizing a "favorite stories" approach and helping each student select and share a favorite story, or act out a story, or write and then share an original story. This activity might then spill over into other areas: the students might decide to re-create with wooden blocks the town in which the story's characters live, or they might decide to paint each of the characters. Any concern a student has can help the teacher break down the barriers of traditionally separate subjects. At the elementary level, a student's interest in snakes can lead to drawings and paintings, songs and stories, charts and statistics, the design of living conditions, or the study of population problems, nutritional requirements, or different cultures.

The teacher may prefer to begin making changes in his methods rather than in subject content. He may find it comfortable to experiment with different kinds of groups (*not* chosen by achievement or ability test scores). At times the whole class could get together for planning; at other times students could break into small groups to plan, consulting the teacher as needed. There might be times when the class gathers together to help some group with a problem it is having in pursuing its goals. At times the class might want to hold meetings to discuss procedural or organizational matters that concern the entire group. Although the class schedule would vary from day to day, students would not become upset by this variation, because they would be involved in the decision-making process and the decisions they reach would be placed where everyone could refer to them—on the blackboard or on a ditto sheet prepared and distributed to each student by a planning committee.

The teacher may prefer instead to experiment with independent study for volunteers or to set aside an independent work period during a class or during parts of the day. He will need to be flexible with this approach, since students differ in terms of the length of time and the time of day that they can work productively in independent study.

Sometimes it is easier for the teacher to facilitate self-directed learning by devoting a small portion of class time during the first week of his transition to talking with students about the things that interest and concern them (87). He could ask them what they would most enjoy doing in the class and what they would be willing to commit themselves to doing on their own for a short period of time, e.g., twenty minutes. If his students have difficulty making a selection and committing themselves to an activity, the teacher could make suggestions or bring to class some of his own books and materials or perhaps present them with options that he believes would interest them. He could also ask his students to bring to class objects, reading materials, pictures, and games that interest them, and he could talk with them about the events in their lives that they value most. Herbert Kohl employed these techniques successfully with his thirty-six children (88).

I brought part of my library to school and temporarily substituted it for social studies. The children were curious about those Greeks and Latins who contributed so many words and concepts to our language. I brought in books on Greek and Roman architecture and art, as well as Robert Graves's version of the *Iliad,* a paperback translation of Apuleius' *Cupid and Psyche,* the *Larousse Encyclopedia of Mythology,* and anything else that seemed relevant or interesting. I showed the books to the children and let them disappear into their desks. It was made clear that the books were to be read, the pages to be turned. If someone reads a book so intensely that the book is bruised it is flattering to the book.

For three-quarters of an hour a day the Parthenon circulated along with Floyd Patterson and J. D. Salinger, Partridge's dictionary of word origins made its way through the class with

Langston Hughes and the Bobbsey twins. Anything I could get my hands on was brought to class—a great deal remained unread, and some books I hadn't read myself shocked and surprised the class. They were sexy and popular. Later that year my supervisor told me I was running a very effective individualized reading program. That may have been it, but the truth seemed simpler and less structured. I overwhelmed the class with books, many of which I loved, and let them discover for themselves what they liked. There were no reports to be written, no requirements about numbers of pages to be read. Some children hardly read at all, others devoured whatever was in the room. The same is true of my friends.

Robert Jackson grabbed a book on Greek architecture, copied floor plans and perspective drawings, and finally, leaping out of the book, created a reasonably accurate scale model of the Parthenon. Alvin and Michael built a clay volcano, asked for and got a chemistry book which showed them how to simulate an eruption. Sam, Thomas, and Dennis fought their way through war books; through the Navy, the Seabees, the Marines, and the Paratroops. The girls started with the Bobbsey twins and worked through to romantic novels and, in the case of a few, Thurber and O. Henry. I learned that there were no books to fear, and having been divested of my fear of idleness, I also wasn't worried if some children went through periods of being unable to do anything at all. . . .

I had brought many things from home for the children; now they brought things for me to learn from. Some brought in a Moms Mabley record and from the other children's reaction it was obvious that she was "in." I had never heard of her and asked the class who she was. They all volunteered information; that she was ancient, funny, and nice, that she liked young boys and kids, that people lined up on 125th Street whenever she was at the Apollo Theater, that she sounded on people in the audience.

We listened to Moms, the class explaining the jokes, translating some of her dialect for me. It pleased them to be listened to. After that we kept a phonograph in the room, and the children brought in the latest records. We listened to them together at the end of the morning or the afternoon. I transcribed the words and every once in a while put them on the blackboard and discussed what the songs were all about.

. . . Music became an integral part of the classroom. The children brought in their records; I responded with my own. One morn-ing I put twenty-five records ranging from blues and Fats Waller through Thelonious Monk and Coltrane to Mozart and Beethoven on top of the phonograph. During the morning breaks the kids explored freely, and when the music began to interest some indi-viduals enough, I brought in biographies of the composers, pic-tures of the musicians. We talked in small groups during social studies of chain gangs, field music, modern jazz, rock and roll, child prodigies, anything that came up. A dialogue between the children and myself was developing. [Pp. 39–40, 44]

In addition to bringing to class magazines, records, and other objects they value, the class could visit relevant places outside the school that they believe might relate to specific topics and problems in their subject. In rural areas there are insects, rocks, plants, small animals, lakes, and so on. In urban areas there are construction sites, hospitals, shops, power plants, office buildings, police stations, transportation facilities. In many urban areas there are also museums, zoos, airports, train terminals, missions, harbors, libraries, et cetera. All of these and more can be used as a basis for planning specific activities and projects in the class-room—readings, paintings, music, construction of tools, equip-ment and models, simulations of social problems, experiments— that utilize a variety of media.

Perhaps the teacher would like to start by bringing to class a variety of *human* resources. He could invite people from all walks of life (business, politics, medicine, law, sports) to come to class and talk about their lives and jobs and share some of their experi-ences and skills. The students could be encouraged to ask what-ever questions they want about the person's occupation, skills, and experiences—what he likes to do most and why, how he decided to do some of the things he has done or is now doing, what he would most like to work toward or achieve, and how they could acquire some of the skills and experience he has acquired. The teacher might later suggest the option of visiting the places where these and other people work. Wherever there is a person with special interests, knowledge, or skills or wherever there is a place that provides a unique opportunity for discovering, that person or place is a valuable resource for learning and should be utilized. A "community resource file" listing each of the people in the community who can share their time, knowledge, and skills for a period of time each week or month would be a very valuable aid.

In English classes the teacher may find it appropriate to begin making changes in his classroom by providing his students with the option of writing and producing a class newspaper or television program or radio broadcast, making use of problems, issues, and concepts in a particular subject.

The social studies teacher could suggest that his students consider organizing themselves as a social-action group and try to come to grips with a local social problem. Or he might prefer to explore the possible use of simulations or games that deal with propaganda, war, race, money, and so on.

Materials salvaged from neighborhood scrap piles or environmental recycling centers can be a starting point in mathematics or science classes. A few such items might be discarded toys, magnets, batteries, the motor of a car, a radio, a typewriter, a toaster, or an adding machine. Discarded furniture and equipment used by such specialized groups as doctors, dentists, nurses, plumbers, or masons also provide many opportunities for exploring and for sparking students' interests in different activities (93).

The teacher needs to keep in mind, however, that merely collecting materials will not ensure that students will plan and conduct valuable classroom activities. In many elementary classrooms teachers have accumulated enormous amounts of materials: they have filled numerous shelves with attractively displayed reading materials; they have designed eye-catching bulletin boards; they have displayed pictures with thought-provoking captions; they have provided science tables with carefully labeled specimens and an aquarium well stocked with beautiful fish; and they have made available typewriters, cassette and tape recorders, magnets, and batteries. Yet the students, after examining the materials, were unable to plan and follow through on a project or task. Besides making materials and equipment available, the teacher needs to engage the students in the use of problem-solving skills with the collected materials for a specific period of time. The students must engage in the processes of comparing, hypothesizing, testing, and generalizing.

The teacher can get a youngster started with a question such as, "Would you like to find out which materials you can pick up with a magnet? Maybe you could list on a sheet of paper all the different materials you use the magnet with and place a 'yes' after the word on the list if the magnet picks it up and a 'no' after the word if the magnet does not pick it up." While the student is experimenting, the teacher can work with a second student on another activity. Later he can return to the first student and pose another question, such as, "What do you think is the reason why the magnet can pick up some things and not others?"

While the teacher would propose or suggest new options for his students, he would allow them to say No to whatever he suggests regardless of how he personally feels about it. However, the teacher should insist that each student make a choice and commit himself to a constructive activity. He can make it clear that, while the student has the freedom to plan his own learning, he is not freed from making a commitment. The teacher also makes it clear that he will make himself available and provide whatever resources he can to help each student complete his project, although he will not tell him *how* to complete it.

Predictably, as the teacher first begins to experiment with the shared classroom, new problems need to be solved, established work patterns will need to be modified, and new techniques will need to be developed. The classroom will be less organized and less logical from an external viewpoint. A vast array of materials will be brought in or produced by students. However, this is the nature of a responsive learning environment—there is openness, activity, inquiry, variety, and experimentation. This is how the teacher and students respond when they are continually caught up in the excitement of searching for new meanings and competencies.

The teacher who wants to discover more effective ways of facilitating self-directed learning in a shared classroom must also search for fresh approaches to teaching outside the classroom.

To encourage the development of new ideas, the teacher may find the following suggestions helpful (30):

1. Read in fields outside your own. This will broaden your perspective on solving problems and making innovations. Start with closely related fields and gradually move on to less related areas. As you read in each area, continually ask yourself, "Could I make some use of this in my classroom? How?" Take notes while you read, recording any idea or suggestion that holds some possible use for you.

2. Always carry a note pad and pen with you. Ideas occur at any hour and often under unusual circumstances. You need to jot them down on the spot. Don't rely on your memory. One often loses a good idea because he thinks he will remember it, only to discover a short while later that it has slipped away.

3. Engage in activities such as chess, bridge, and puzzle-solving. Since these activities often help you relax as you employ problem-solving skills, free associations are facilitated and new ways of doing things frequently come to mind.

4. Organize your time with long periods when you can be completely alone and silent. You need to have a chance to analyze your ideas without distraction.

5. Never accept any assumption about how a problem originated or how it "must" be solved. Assumptions are usually treated as self-evident truths and therefore often kill one's search for new ideas and new ways of solving problems. Always question how and why something is so.

6. Look for relationships between things that others have discounted. Pursue any unorthodox or unusual approach, even if the facts don't seem to warrant it. Keep on speculating and guessing. Don't try to demonstrate how impractical a new approach is. Think of minor changes that would make it work.

7. Don't kill your own ideas by saying to people you want to influence or persuade, "This may not work, but——" or "I don't know whether you would like to give this much

consideration, but——" or "Do you suppose it would be possible to——" or "It may take a long time, but——"

8. Recognize when others are killing your ideas and destroying your confidence in yourself, e.g., when they say, "We've never done it that way before"; "It won't work"; "What will the other teachers think?"; "You don't understand our problem"; "Let's form a committee"; "Let's wait and see"; "Let's put it in writing"; "It's not in the manual"; "That takes money and we haven't got it." The teacher who wants to change must be especially alert to this last idea-killer. Continually bear in mind that most of the new ideas and practices that are needed to help our young people direct their own learning do not require huge outlays of money. They simply require teachers who desire change and who go about the job of putting their ideas into practice.

Obviously, a teacher can move toward conducting a shared classroom more easily when he receives some effective help and support from others. Unfortunately, the student preparing to become a teacher may find that his training, especially his student teaching experience, does not help him acquire the skills to operate a shared classroom. While the student teacher is eager to put into practice the new techniques he may have heard described and seen demonstrated in his courses on methods or educational psychology, he quickly discovers when he enters the classroom that the degree to which he is able to try out what he has conceptualized depends on the kind of cooperating teacher and supervisor he has. On the one hand, if the student teacher has a "co-op" who is perceptive, flexible, and supportive, he will receive the freedom and guidance he needs to become the best teacher he can become —thus proving that an apprenticeship with a skilled and human co-op is the single most relevant and effective pre-service opportunity for becoming a competent teacher. On the other hand, if the student teacher has an insecure, rigid, and dogmatic co-op, his student teaching experience can be an agonizing and terribly frustrating one, perhaps even one that kills his desire to teach.

The student teacher will most likely make similar discoveries about his supervisor. His supervisor may provide him with the freedom and guidance he needs to develop a constructive teaching style according to his own sense of himself. Or, his supervisor may be unaware or afraid of the new ideas the student teacher has acquired and unwilling to permit him to experiment with a shared classroom approach. The student teacher may very well be told by his supervisor, "Your place is in front of the room and not on students' desks or in small groups, or fooling around with teaching fads."

Although the student teaching experience may be quite discouraging, a person's chances of designing and conducting a shared classroom improve when he becomes a certified and salaried teacher. A first-year teacher has far more freedom to develop a shared classroom than does a student teacher, and his freedom increases with each year he stays on at a school.

The neophyte, however, must appreciate the dynamics of school administration. When the young teacher starts to teach, he may find that the principal of his school is forced to concern himself primarily with finance and public relations, not with operating shared classrooms. Some—perhaps most—of the programs and practices in his school will have been instituted mainly to economize or to placate certain pressure groups, not to facilitate self-directed learning.

The principal may in effect say to the new teacher, "Keep your nose clean and you will get along well here." There is often a temptation for a new teacher, excited about change, to confront the administration. However, as a general rule, the new teacher should not set himself against the school principal. If an entire school is to change, the principal must receive support and not opposition. Obviously, the principal has to be in favor of change if there is to be reform; however, he cannot be required to bring it about by himself or to offer himself as a sacrificial lamb to parents, school boards, and taxpayers. The teacher must bear in mind that the principal is always in an extremely vulnerable position, with different factions pressuring him, perhaps even clawing at him with threats to cut off money or have him fired if he does not accede to their wishes or fears. While the principal may be the major cause of educational failure in some schools, it is unfair and unrealistic to expect him to carry the entire burden of educational reform.

Principals do not have unions or organizations, as teachers do, to protect their rights and support their efforts at innovation. Consequently, few principals are willing to take risks with new teaching approaches unless they have the majority of the faculty supporting their recommendations. If a teacher wants his principal to change, he must first change himself, then find another teacher and together find a third and so on until they have a sizable group to give the principal support in recommending change to the school board.

Often the only support a new teacher needs is one other teacher in the building who will join in his efforts. For example, two teachers can collaborate to exchange students for a class or part of a day and have the students teach other students in their classes. The teachers should then let other teachers and the principal see that a student does not have to know or do something perfectly to help another student learn; that slow learners, gifted students, and so-called problem students can teach each other something and get along well together; and that even the "hopeless" student can often improve his rate of learning when he works with younger students. An administrator will often grab the opportunity to make his school a showcase and be able to tell parents that his teachers are innovative yet sensible and that "they are also saving the taxpayers' money."

At first the teacher may discover that designing a shared classroom is a lonely, difficult experience. He must be convinced that the benefits to students far outweigh the obstacles and frustrations he may encounter. He must also recognize that he will need help to effect change—help from students to run the class, help and suggestions from in-service programs, continuing workshops, and other teachers to improve his teaching skills and the quality of school administration, and perhaps help from skilled clinicians to learn more about himself.

Further, the teacher must recognize that deception, although sometimes effective, is a dangerous way of trying to bring about change. He cannot use two different lesson plans—an innovative one for his class and a traditional one for the front office—without implying to his students and other teachers that deception is justified. This implication can harm the entire school and sharply reduce the teacher's influence on others. Although the development of a shared classroom is a difficult journey in almost any school, it must be brought about honestly if the teacher wants his students to learn that dishonesty and deceit are unacceptable ways to solve problems.

If the school doesn't want the kind of changes the teacher believes in, he must still go ahead and try some things out, but he must make small changes, one at a time, and show one other teacher how it can work in his classroom. He must not try to make a massive change by himself. He will only be threatening other teachers and the administration and get himself fired, and that won't do his students any good.

Many teachers are moving toward the development of a shared classroom at the elementary and secondary levels, and they are doing it honestly. Here are five teachers who give their accounts of trying to plan and implement reality-oriented classroom activities and help their students engage in self-directed learning within the context of a shared environment.

One teacher is Michael Thatcher, who describes how he approached a unit on writing poetry with his high school students (162). Thatcher recognized that poetry as it is commonly taught in high school is far removed from students' lives. He found, however, that popular music is a vital part of students' out-of-school experience and so "it's a good place to begin." After pointing out how poetry and music historically have always been interdependent—e.g., the cross-fertilization of music and literature involving the works of Schubert and Beethoven—he asked his classes to suggest songwriters and poets they would like to study. From each class he got a comprehensive list of names—"names," as he recalls, "that I would have chosen myself" (Bob Dylan, Simon and Garfunkel, the Beatles). In planning poetry-writing sessions he let the students select the artists and he selected the songs. After an artist and song were selected, Thatcher would pass out copies of the song and the class would listen to it and try to discover "what it meant and *how* it meant"; the students' search for the song's meaning led them to examine concepts such as imagery and figurative language. After the students analyzed a few songs, Thatcher would then present together two songs that had a similar message in order to convey the concept of "thematic continuity." For example, he compared the Beatles' "Fixing a Hole" and "Fool on the Hill."

He found that the comparative approach was a good way to introduce virtually any kind of poem: when the class compared the two Beatles songs, he introduced Wordsworth's sonnet "The World Is Too Much With Us," and he led the class to compare all three as rejections of society. Later the class made comparisons between Simon and Garfunkel's "Dangling Conversation" and George Meredith's sonnets *Modern Love,* and many other poems and popular songs. Gradually his students began to write their own poems or songs while they studied matters such as line length, stanza, organization, use of repeated lines, phrases, rhyme, meter, and other elements of poems they could identify. Thatcher also collaborated with the music teacher, who agreed to have his music students help Thatcher's students set some of their poems to music.

For their final activity in this unit, the students selected a song or poem of their choice and wrote an analysis of it, considering its setting, the speaker, the audience, the poetic devices, the tone, and the message. "They were caught up in the assignment. . . . By the end of the unit . . . my students and I had learned something about the language of poetry, and I was heartened by their enthusiasm; they had found that poetry is not just a pastime for old ladies and schoolteachers, but a fascinating part of their everyday experience."

Thatcher began his movement toward a shared classroom by breaking down the barriers between what have often been two separate courses in a high school curriculum. Then he and his students experimented with one unit for a few weeks. They shared in the decision-making, and he provided as much help as the students needed in order to reach the point where they could plan and conduct a major classroom activity on their own.

Janelle Barlow began her movement toward a shared classroom in each of her four high school social studies classes with simulations (6). Her goal was to let her students discover how governmental institutions conduct their business and to help them learn to deal more constructively with emotion-laden social questions. In one simulation, a mock Congress was designed in each of her classes, with students grouping themselves as either Democrats or Republicans and members of either the Senate or the House.

After students learned about the procedure involved in having bills become laws, each class conducted a simulation of the legislative process. Barlow alerted her students at the outset that conducting a simulation was not only for the purpose of having fun. If a fun-only attitude developed and went unchecked, a few students might spoil the simulation for the entire class. Barlow monitored students' efforts carefully, and she felt free to break in when a difficulty arose and explain the point at issue or clarify where the students were and what was still to be considered.

As a follow-up to their simulations, students would take the bills used in class and determine whether or not a particular piece of legislation would actually get through Congress and why. Through group discussion on these and related matters, Barlow was able to determine what each student had learned for himself about the real structure and procedures of Congress: that extremely controversial pieces of legislation are often killed or bottlenecked in committee; that most of the business conducted by Congress takes place in committee; that the chairmen of various committees have enormous power; and that the House Rules Committee is an extremely important group.

Barlow's classes also found it relevant to conduct some simulations of intergroup conflicts and social problems, specifically, one dealing with the integration of a white neighborhood by a black family. Each student was provided with a sheet describing the neighborhood involved and its homes, the investments in the community that each homeowner had to protect, the various concerned groups and organizations in the community and their position on the integration issue, and the specific interactional events that were to occur. Interested students then elected to represent either an organization to "protect property values," or a civil rights group, or the P.T.A., or the real estate company that sold the property, or the local Chamber of Commerce.

On the day of the actual simulation, a number of spontaneous events occurred in class, including an emotional debate, a sit-down strike, a series of arrests (an empty classroom was used as the jail), and the printing and distributing of several "newspaper" articles and propaganda sheets. It was also reported in the local "newspaper" that the black family's home had been attacked and that the real estate men had received threatening phone calls.

When the simulation was completed, it was discovered that three of the four classes were unable to solve the integration problem. The class that was successful had set up private conferences with the negotiators on each side, making every effort to reach an accord. However, through follow-up discussions, the classes that had "failed" to resolve the problem were able to discover many of the reasons why they and our society find the integration issue a difficult one. Also, all the classes discovered that their experience provided a valuable reference point when they examined other social issues and studied a unit of black history.

Some adverse public opinion did develop as the result of Barlow's simulations, in the form of two telephone calls to the principal charging that the school was being used for "demonstration" purposes. Barlow recalls, "We countered by calling the local newspaper, which then wrote a . . . letter praising the use of simulations as a learning device." She also points out that the support she received from the faculty members and the chairman of the social studies department helped to make the simulations successful. What did the students think about the simulations? Barlow found this approach to learning to be "one of the more successful devices for getting students to the point where they are not only capable but also willing, indeed eager, to draw their own conclusions."

As a first-year mathematics teacher, Bonnie Mathisen established her major goals: (*1*) to motivate each student to want to learn and (*2*) to devise an accurate way of evaluating each student's day-to-day understanding and skills (102). To achieve them, Mathisen first examined the textbooks at her school and discovered that they did not emphasize the more fascinating aspects of mathematics for her seventh- and eighth-grade students. Consequently, she found supplementary materials and chose techniques to allay students' fears about math and to capture their interest and imagination. She decided also to allow students to work either alone, in pairs, or in small groups.

As one of her techniques, Mathisen tried a number of math experiments involving the use of shapes and forms and found them highly effective in helping students learn area relationships. In one experiment the students rearranged plane figures to form squares and to find the areas contained in triangles, parallelograms, trapezoids, and other figures.

Mathisen found a variety of math-oriented games effective in helping her students understand mathematical concepts. She designed her own math games (e.g., cross-number games and games using dice) and had students make up clues to puzzles for the class to solve. She found dice games especially effective for teaching place value, for understanding bases, and for introducing new mathematical concepts.

She had frequent class discussions to be continually aware of her students' current feelings and skills. She also used "reflection sheets" to give students an opportunity each Friday to tell her what they did not understand in math for the week. They wrote what they liked or disliked about the class, what they had done that they were proud of, or how they disappointed themselves or others. The sheets gave each student in the class the opportunity to exchange ideas and feelings and to consider his plans and commitments for upcoming weeks.

Mathisen found that these methods helped her to achieve both of her goals. Since her techniques required the student and not the teacher to be the major performer, she found that her students were always involved and that they were discovering "all by themselves." Self-directed discovery on the part of students in turn freed her to observe each student's performance carefully. Her method of teaching mathematics made it far more possible for her to get immediate and very comprehensive feedback about each student's progress and to determine exactly what the student understood and could do and where he needed to direct his energies.

Bonnie Mathisen's techniques "worked well," and she discovered, as did Janelle Barlow and Michael Thatcher, that a subject can be made a concrete, interesting, and satisfying experience for both teacher and student.

Another teacher who has taken some steps toward developing a shared classroom is June Masters, who recounts her first year of teaching biology at a "tough" school, Castlemont High School in Oakland, California (101).

When Masters attended faculty conferences before September classes began, she was terrified about expected discipline problems and the riots that might break out during the coming school year. (Castlemont was labeled a "problem" school because of its 90 per cent black population.) She, like every other teacher, was issued a thick manual of rules and regulations she was expected to enforce.

She had forty-five students enrolled in her largest section and thirty in her smallest. Three of her five classes were considered "slow," and the other two were viewed as "average." She met her classes, checked roll and admission cards, described what the students would be doing during the semester, and gave her little speech about being responsible, self-disciplined, mature people.

At first Masters took the position that the students must be ready and motivated. She began the course by using the Biological Sciences Curriculum Study special materials *Patterns and Processes* for the three slow classes and *Elements of Biology* for the other two. The students were not responding. She tried punishing, "ranting and raving," but that did not help. She discovered from her analysis of the books and the way she had set up her classes that students were bored. She also recognized that much of the content was boring to her as well (an admission few teachers are willing to make). It dawned on her that she was the one who had to be ready; she had to meet students' needs. She revised her plans and materials and, most importantly, she gave students some responsibility in gathering their own materials. As Masters recalls, "It worked wonders."

Soon she was swamped with spiders of all descriptions, frogs, toads, moths, turtles, snakes, lizards, snails, slugs, fish. The biology room was "a hum of activity." One day she brought in some mice and the class spent nearly all day watching the snake eat six of them. The students had to be extremely quiet or the snake would not eat. No one spoke for the entire period, and as the students left, some positioned themselves near the doorway to caution the incoming class against making noise. It was the quietest day she ever had.

The most exciting experiment of all was when the class tested the behavior patterns of some lower animals. The students brought earthworms, fish, and an assortment of snails and turtles whose responses were tested with electricity, light, and chemicals such as salt and weak acid. Masters notes, "When the period ended I could hardly get them to stop."

Discipline problems? Today Masters has "very few, if any, because there is a mutual respect between teacher and student, and, more importantly, the students are involved in what is going on."

An important point about the preceding accounts is that each concerns the efforts of a first-year teacher. None of the teachers was a seasoned veteran with a wealth of teaching experience to draw on; yet with imagination and courage each was able to demonstrate that beginning teachers can do some remarkably good things in the classroom.

It is also important to note that each of these teachers was successful in meeting the needs of not one but several classes, and that they met their students for only one period each day. In addition, the four accounts reveal that relevant and personally meaningful learning can occur in *all* areas of education, including the "essentials"—the three R's and the sciences. These teachers made English, social studies, mathematics, and biology come alive in the classroom and related these areas to students' lives.

The final account of successful teaching is a description of Barbara Shiel's efforts in helping her sixth-graders learn to direct their own learning (135). Unlike the teachers in the preceding stories, Shiel is a veteran teacher with classroom experience in each grade at the elementary level.

The thirty-six children she had in her sixth-grade class comprised "one of the most difficult" groups she had ever worked with in terms of discipline and "lack of interest." The students' IQ's ranged from 82 to 135. Several were classified as "socially maladjusted," "underachievers," and "emotionally disturbed." Shiel had exhausted the traditional ways of trying to teach and cope with the array of classroom problems she had, and so during the spring of her thirteenth year of teaching she began her movement toward helping students direct their own learning.

One morning in March she told the class that, as an "experiment," for one day they could do anything they wanted to do or nothing if they so wished. Some read, some did projects in art, and others worked in math and other areas. Many became so interested in what they were doing that when recess or noon arrived they wanted to continue with their activities.

When the students discussed how they thought the one-day experiment went, reactions were mixed, but most felt that the class went extremely well. They felt that they had accomplished at least as much as they had under teacher-controlled conditions and that they had accomplished it without being "forced" to learn.

While some students were confused by not being given specific assignments and told how to do them, most students "begged" to continue the experiment. There was agreement to continue the experiment for two more days, after which time the class would evaluate the results.

During the next two-day period, Shiel employed a "work contract" to help students plan and organize their activities. She prepared and distributed ditto sheets on which were listed a wide range of subjects and the suggested activities in each of them. Each student drew up his contract for the day by selecting each of the areas in which he wanted to work and each of the activities he would complete. On the ditto sheet there was space for each student to state his "plans" in each area and to record the completion of each activity.

Upon completing an activity, the student was to check his own work, using the teacher's manual where appropriate. All of his work was to be kept in a folder with his contract. Shiel also met with each student to discuss his plans, progress, and achievements. She helped him make an adjustment in his plans when they did not appear to be challenging, e.g., by suggesting that additional materials or areas might be included in his daily contract.

Discipline continued to be a great problem during the three-day experiment, with some students demonstrating less "self-control" than before the experiment began. However, she recognized that there were more "problems" simply because the children could sit where and with whom they preferred and express feelings and ideas that previously were not permitted to be a part of classroom life. Consequently, there were arguments and occasional fights. More problems had to be expected at first if students were to be free to express their individuality, look at their feelings and ideas, and begin to make their own decisions about how to harness them in constructive ways. Shiel kept reminding herself that, although some students may have been quieter under the old program, they had completed fewer activities.

She considered the possibility of "reestablishing her control" but realized that she would be defeating one of the basic goals of the program. She felt that if she could stay with the class during this trying period of openness of feelings and ideas, the students would develop great self-control.

When the class evaluated the entire three-day experiment, the overwhelming majority were enthusiastic about the different approach to learning. Shiel asked the few students who still felt insecure and wanted specific assignments if they would give themselves and the experiment more time. They consented, and the class was excited at the expectation of directing their own learning for the rest of the year.

A couple of days later Shiel realized that under the present plan she was expecting too much too soon from some students. Several students continued to feel frustrated and insecure without teacher direction and were unable or unwilling to assume total responsibility for directing their own learning at that time. Moreover, their inability to assume self-direction was disrupting those who wanted to and could direct their own learning. The whole class was being penalized. So Shiel decided to modify the program by organizing a large group for students who wanted to and could assume responsibility for self-direction and a small group for students who for various reasons were unable to engage effectively in self-directed learning.

She continued to require each student to design his own personal learning contract each day, specifying the area in which he would work and the activities he would commit himself to completing. She explained that she was not free to discard the state-devised weekly time–subject blocks and that this was to be a consideration in their planning. She also helped them to understand sequential learning, especially in math—i.e., that it was important to master some skills at one level in order to be successful in acquiring skills at a higher level. She pointed out that the text and other materials provided an introduction to specific skills, demonstrated the skills, suggested skill-developing exercises, and provided tests to check achievement. She informed them about the various films and other resources available to her and how on some days either the entire class or a group of students could draw up a work plan. She also asked each student to continue to keep his own work folder, to evaluate his own work, and to discuss his work with her after self-evaluation. She also reminded her students that when they found that they were having no difficulty at all completing their activities, it might mean that their work was not challenging enough and that perhaps their work contract needed to be revised.

After a student drew up his contract, he began his planned activities and worked as long as he needed or wanted to work. He began at his own level, set his own pace, and went as far as he wished or was able to go. When he felt he was ready to go on to another area or plan another contract, he was free to do so. If students wanted to share the fruits of their work or if they felt that it was necessary to discuss individual, group, or class problems, they could arrange desks and tables to do so.

Shiel found that, at the end of their first week with the new classroom approach, the group of self-directed students had made greater strides, learning how to program their work and teach themselves (and each other). Several students had completed the year's "required" work in some of the areas, such as spelling. She also found that when students were directing their own learning she had a great deal of time to talk and work with individual students and small groups.

At the end of the second week, she held an individual conference with each student to discuss his general progress and feelings. She discovered that several of the students in the teacher-directed group felt that they were ready to go into the self-directed group. They wanted the freedom to direct their own learning and they believed that they understood and could assume the responsibilities involved. It was decided that they would try it for one week to see if they really were ready. She would help them at any time they needed help in planning their contract and in conducting their activities. At this point six children remained in the teacher-directed group.

During the next three-week period she found that several students continued to feel insecure and frustrated without her guidance. They needed a great deal of help, and she provided it, but she also arranged a period every day during which each of them could assume some responsibility for self-direction. After five weeks of her experiment with the class, only four students remained in the teacher-directed group.

The experiment continued until the end of the spring term. As the month of June approached she found that *all* students —gifted, slow, underachievers—had made enormous progress. She was especially impressed by the "slow learners." Some who had been unable to retain the multiplication tables were able to multiply and divide fractions with very few errors. They had learned to evaluate their own progress in each area and to determine the degree to which they had fulfilled their commitments. They learned that the number of mistakes a person made was not the standard for determining his failure or success. They discovered that failure was "only a word," that there was a difference between failure and making mistakes, and that mistakes are a part of the learning process. Since evaluation was self-initiated and respected by the teacher, she found that students did not need to cheat to achieve success.

They had developed values, attitudes, and standards of behavior on their own, and they had lived up to those standards. Although they still argued and fought, there was a definite change. The frequency of quarrels and outbursts had diminished. Other teachers and playground supervisors seldom had to discipline them. They too had recognized a change in the students' behavior and attitudes.

As she reflected on the experience, Shiel recalled how on some days she felt confident, buoyant, sure that she and the students were on the right track. On other days she found that all of her pre-service training and the entire authoritarian tradition in education "threatened and intimidated her."

She came to realize that "one must be secure in his own self-concept to undertake such a program. In order to relinquish the accepted role of the teacher in a teacher-directed program, one must understand and accept oneself first."

She also found that to succeed she had to make a commitment. She had to see her methods and ideas not merely as gimmicks but as essential to provide each student with the opportunity for self-growth—not only creativity, initiative, imagination, but self-discipline, self-acceptance, and understanding. She found that while several other teachers tried to do what she did, they were unsuccessful "primarily, I think, because they did not really believe in it."

There are many reasons why a teacher becomes successful in helping his students learn to direct their own learning, and the specific approach relevant and effective in one classroom may not produce success in another. The preceding personal accounts by five teachers indicate that each teacher must understand himself and discover in his own way the materials and methods he needs to use and the kind of relationship he needs to establish with his students to help them become self-directed learners. The rate at which he feels secure and competent enough to make the needed changes will also vary from teacher to teacher. For some teachers it is most advantageous to make the transition by trying some innovations in only part of their subject or with only some of their methods each year. However, the experimental efforts and success of June Masters and Barbara Shiel demonstrate that the teacher can make the transition in an entire subject or class and within a single school term or year. They also demonstrated that the amount of time available to meet with students is not so important as the classroom methods used.

When students share in the selection of learning events and when the content of learning is based on what the student brings to the classroom—his skills and knowledge, his fears and hopes, his style of discovering and of applying discoveries—learning and teaching can become extremely satisfying in both the self-contained elementary classroom and in the departmentalized high school. And the shared classroom can become a reality in all of our public schools.

APPENDICES

Appendix A

Clues for murder mystery Who, How, When, and Where.*

1. When he was discovered dead, Mr. Kelley had a bullet hole in his thigh and a knife wound in his back.
2. Mr. Jones shot at an intruder in his apartment building at 12:00 midnight.
3. The elevator operator reported to police that he saw Mr. Kelley at 12:15 A.M.
4. The bullet taken from Mr. Kelley's thigh matched the gun owned by Mr. Jones.
5. Only one bullet had been fired from Mr. Jones's gun.
6. When the elevator man saw Mr. Kelley, Mr. Kelley was bleeding slightly, but he did not seem too badly hurt.
7. A knife with Mr. Kelley's blood on it was found in Miss Smith's yard.
8. The knife found in Miss Smith's yard had Mr. Scott's fingerprints on it.
9. Mr. Kelley had destroyed Mr. Jones's business by stealing all his customers.
10. The elevator man saw Mr. Kelley's wife go to Mr. Scott's apartment at 11:30 P.M.

* From G. Stanford and B. D. Stanford, *Learning Discussion Skills Through Games* (New York: Citation Press, 1969), pp. 24–26. Reprinted by permission of the publisher.

11. The elevator operator said that Mr. Kelley's wife frequently left the building with Mr. Scott.
12. Mr. Kelley's body was found in the park.
13. Mr. Kelley's body was found at 1:30 A.M.
14. Mr. Kelley had been dead for one hour when his body was found, according to a medical expert working with police.
15. The elevator man saw Mr. Kelley go to Mr. Scott's room at 12:25 A.M.
16. The elevator man went off duty at 12:30 A.M.
17. It was obvious from the condition of Mr. Kelley's body that it had been dragged a long distance.
18. Miss Smith saw Mr. Kelley go to Mr. Jones's apartment building at 11:55 P.M.
19. Mr. Kelley's wife disappeared after the murder.
20. Police were unable to locate Mr. Scott after the murder.
21. When police tried to locate Mr. Jones after the murder, they discovered that he had disappeared.
22. The elevator man said that Miss Smith was in the lobby of the apartment building when he went off duty.
23. Miss Smith often followed Mr. Kelley.
24. Mr. Jones had told Mr. Kelley that he was going to kill him.
25. Miss Smith said that nobody left the apartment building between 12:25 A.M and 12:45 A.M.
26. Mr. Kelley's blood stains were found in Mr. Scott's car.
27. Mr. Kelley's blood stains were found on the carpet in the hall outside Mr. Jones's apartment.

The answer to the murder mystery is that after Mr. Kelley received a superficial gunshot wound from Mr. Jones he went to Mr. Scott's apartment where he was killed by Mr. Scott at 12:30 A.M. with a knife. (The teacher may find that his students are very curious about the motive for the murder, in which case he can have them debate the possibilities.)

Appendix B

The following is an annotated list of some of the simulations and games available commercially. (Also ask publishers to place your name on their mailing lists to inform you of their most current materials.)

Adventuring (Social Studies and History: Junior High)
Deals with the social structure of seventeenth-century England as a prelude to the English Civil War. Students learn about social climbing and various political and social forces. Two related simulations are *The English Civil War Unit* and *Revolution*. Abt Associates, Inc., 55 Wheeler St., Cambridge, Mass. 02136.

Association (Sociology: Senior High–Adult)
Leads students to understand how social and psychological factors operate in the formation of associations among people of the same social class. Western Publishing Company, 850 Third Ave., New York, N.Y. 10022.

Atlantis (Social Studies and History: Upper Elementary–Senior High)
Helps students, playing role of archeologists, learn about an ancient civilization. Portola Institute, 1115 Merrill Street, Menlo Park, Calif. 94025.

BMG (Economics and Social Studies: Junior–Senior High)
Simulates a competitive situation in the marketplace, with students
learning about price, production, advertising, competition, and selling.
Western Behavioral Sciences Institute, 1121 Torrey Pines Blvd., La
Jolla, Calif. 92037.

Bushman Exploring and Gathering (Social Studies: Fifth Grade)
A two-phase board game designed to teach fifth-graders the concept
of cultural adaptation to a harsh environment. Illustrates the subsis-
tence economy of Bushmen in the Kalahari Desert. Available with
Caribou Hunting and *Seal Hunting* for the program "Man—A Course
of Study." Education Development Center, Inc., 15 Mifflin Place,
Cambridge, Mass. 02138.

Campaign (History and Problems of Democracy: Junior High–
        Adult)
Simulates the nomination and election of state legislators, including
campaign tactics, the development of voter issues, and news coverage.
Instructional Simulations, Inc., 2147 University Ave., St. Paul, Minn.
55114.

Caribou Hunting (Social Studies: Elementary)
Deals with some of the difficulties Eskimos experience in hunting
caribou. Cf. *Bushman Exploring and Gathering*. Educational Development Center.

The Cities Game (Social Studies, Problems of Democracy: Soci-
        ology: Junior–Senior High)
Students simulate an attempt by business leaders, slum dwellers, agi-
tators, and government officials to form coalitions to solve social
problems. The Cities Game, 1330 Camino Del Mar, Del Mar, Calif.
92014.

Colony (History: Junior–Senior High)
Simulates relations between the American colonies and Great Britain
during the period after the French and Indian War, when Britain
faced a huge war debt and the problem of increased costs in administering and defending its colonies. Science Research Associates,
259 East Erie St., Chicago, Ill. 60611.

The Columbia River Game (Social Studies: Fourth–Fifth Grade)
Helps students understand the interrelationships of industry, farming,

and the Columbia River. Teaching Research, A Division of the Oregon State System of Higher Education, Monmouth, Ore. 97361.

Community Response (Social Studies, Sociology: Junior High–
Adult)
Builds an understanding of some of the problems individuals face when a community is hit by a natural disaster. Western Publishing Company.

Compass–Community Priority Assessment Simulation (Social
Studies and Sociology: Junior High–Adult)
Key city groups attempt to implement a model-city plan. Students represent area power groups and organizations. Instructional Simulations.

Consumer (Economics and Sociology: Senior High–Adult)
Simulates the consumer buying process, including competition among installment buyers and credit agents. Western Publishing Company.

Crisis (Social Studies: Junior–Senior High)
A simplified version of *Inter-National Simulation*. Students representing different nations attempt to resolve their international disputes. Western Behavioral Sciences Institute.

Crithaka (Social Studies: Upper Elementary)
This simulation is based on the social system of the Kikuyus of Kenya and attempts to help students understand how people attempt to improve their status within a class. The Learning Center, Social Studies Department, Princeton, N.J. 08540.

Dangerous Parallel (Social Studies, History, International Affairs:
Senior High–Adult)
Students experience the process of formulating policies and making foreign-policy decisions when facing a conflict similar to the Korean War. Scott, Foresman & Co., 1900 E. Lake Ave., Glenview, Ill. 60025.

Democracy (Legislature) (Problems of Democracy and Social
Studies: Junior–Senior High)
Students simulate various aspects of the legislative process of Congress with a set of eight games. Western Publishing Company.

Development (Social Studies: Junior–Senior High)
Two major powers compete for the loyalty of developing countries. The developing countries seek to improve their economy with the help

of the major powers without forfeiting their political independence. Science Research Associates.

Disunia (History and Social Studies: Junior–Senior High)
The setting of this game is a new planet in the year 2087. Students resolve problems similar to those that faced Americans during the period 1781–89. Interact, P.O. Box 202, Lakeside, Calif. 92040.

Economic System (Economics and Social Studies: Junior–Senior High)
Students assuming the roles of workers, manufacturers, and farmers employ principles of economics to advance their profits and standard of living. Western Publishing Company.

Economy (Social Studies: Sixth Grade)
Assuming the roles of machine-shop owners, manufacturers, heads of families, and bankers, students study the circular flow of goods and services in the economic system. Abt Associates.

Election (Social Studies: Upper Elementary–Senior High)
Students simulate the careers of politicians and employ procedures involved in the election of a U.S. President. Educational Games Company, P.O. Box 363, Peekskill, N.Y. 10566.

Empire (Economics and Social Studies: Junior High)
Helps students understand how mercantilism and various economic factors were involved in the transformation of British subjects into Americans. Educational Development Center.

The English Civil War Unit (History: Junior High)
Deals with the question of whether King Charles was a traitor or martyr. Two related simulations are *Adventuring* and *Revolution*. Abt Associates.

Equations (Mathematics: Upper Elementary-Senior High)
Students are encouraged to use arithmetic and algebra. Wff'n Proof, Box 71, New Haven, Conn. 06501.

Free Enterprise (Social Studies: Elementary)
Simulates the free enterprise system and helps students understand the economic principles involved. Board of Cooperative Educational Services, 845 Meadow Road, Yorktown Heights, N.Y. 10598.

Frontier (History: Junior–Senior High)
Focuses on the process of American westward expansion and emphasizes the economic, political, and social differences of the Northwest and Southwest sections of the United States and the role sectional differences played in the development of the Civil War. Science Research Associates.

Galápagos (Social Studies: Junior–Senior High)
Helps students examine factors involved in the evolution of species and asks them to predict future evolutionary patterns. Abt Associates.

Get Set: Reading-Readiness Games (Ages 3–6)
A set of eight games to help children develop sound differentiation, context understanding, and beginning skills in reading:
1. Silly Sentences—context; illustrations only
2. Stopdots—punctuation and phrasing; illustrations only
3. Animal Race—beginning sounds; illustrations and letters
4. Broken Letters—beginning sounds; illustrations and letters
5. Dominoes—letter-sound associations; illustrations and letters
6. Pickafit—context, letter-sound associations; illustrations and letters
7. Picture Words—context, reading; illustrations and words
8. Word Train—reading; illustrations and words.
Houghton Mifflin Company, 110 Tremont St., Boston, Mass. 02107.

Generation Gap (Social Studies: Junior–Senior High)
Simulation to help students gain understanding of the roles and interdependent relationships within the family and how different strategies may be effective for handling conflicts. Western Publishing Company.

Ghetto (Social Studies: Junior–Senior High)
Students simulate the roles of fictional people living under ghetto conditions and seeking to improve their standard of living and their community. Western Publishing Company.

Grand Strategy (Social Studies: Junior High–Adult)
Simulates a wartime crisis situation, requiring students to develop strategies of diplomacy to deal with the crisis. Abt Associates.

Heads Up (Mathematics: Elementary–Senior High)
Offers an entertaining approach in the use of fundamental mathe-

matical operations and equations. E. S. Lowe Co., 27 West 20 St., New York, N.Y. 10011.

Impact—A Community Simulation (Social Studies and Sociology: Junior High–Adult)
Students gain experience in decision-making and problem-solving by simulating the roles of people trying to grapple with community problems. Instructional Simulations.

INS (Inter-National Simulation) (Problems of Democracy and Social Studies: Junior–Senior High)
Students make decisions on matters of foreign policy and international politics by simulating the roles of five decision-makers, including the head of state, a domestic opposition leader, and a foreign-policy adviser. Science Research Associates.

Intervention (History: Junior–Senior High)
Explores America's increasing involvement in foreign affairs after the Spanish-American War, especially with the small Caribbean countries. Science Research Associates.

The Kansas/Nebraska Act (History: Junior High)
Part of the series "United States History Simulation." Instructional Innovations, Redlands, Calif.

Kolkhoz (Social Studies: Junior High)
Designed to help students explore the economic philosophy upon which the collective farm operates. Abt Associates.

Krypto (Mathematics: Elementary–Senior High)
Promotes the development of computational skills by a deck of 52 playing cards. Creative Publications, P.O. Box 328, Palo Alto. Calif. 94302.

Life Career (Economics and Social Studies: Junior–Senior High)
Students learn about certain features of the "labor market," the "education market," and the "marriage market" and how these are related to the distribution of time and work. Western Publishing Company.

Machinist (Senior High)
Attempts to help students learn about the job opportunities and vocational careers that may come up after they leave high school

and the advantages and disadvantages associated with each. Information Systems for Vocational Decisions, Graduate School of Education, Harvard University, Cambridge, Mass.

Manchester (History and Social Studies: Senior High)
A simulation on the Industrial Revolution. Abt Associates.

Market (Social Studies: Sixth Grade)
Students learn about the laws of supply and demand by assuming the roles of consumers and sellers in a grocery store. Abt Associates.

Market Game (Economics and Social Studies: Upper Elementary–Senior High)
Simulates aspects of the free-market economy. Part of "Comparative Economic Systems," *Holt Social Studies Curriculum,* edited by Edwin Fenton. Holt, Rinehart and Winston, Inc., 383 Madison Avenue, New York, N.Y. 10017.

Market Game (Economics and Social Studies: Junior–Senior High)
Students learn about the principles of supply and demand, using wheat as a commodity. Joint Council on Economic Education, 1212 Avenue of the Americas, New York, N.Y. 10036.

Mathematics Games (Upper Elementary–Senior High)
Four math games devised around three familiar devices—cards, dominoes, and spinners—to help students review and practice basic mathematical operations. D. C. Heath & Company, 125 Spring Street, Lexington, Mass. 02173.

Napoli (Social Studies, Problems of Democracy: Junior High–Adult)
A simulation designed to help students understand the interrelationship between the legislative process and the behavior of political parties. Western Behavioral Sciences Institute.

On Sets (Mathematics: Upper Elementary–Senior High)
Students learn set theory and its uses in an entertaining manner. Wff'n Proof.

Pacific Express (Social Studies: Junior–Senior High)
Deals with the building of a transcontinental railroad and helps students study and compare methods for completing the task. Mental Health Research Institute, University of Michigan, Ann Arbor, Mich. 48104.

Panic (Economics, Social Studies, and History: Junior–Senior High)
Students represent members of different economic pressure groups in the United States during the period 1920–40. Interact.

Plans (Social Studies: Senior High)
Designed to give high school students an understanding of the role and methods of pressure groups in shaping federal legislation and the national economy. Western Behavioral Sciences Institute.

Pollution (Social Studies: Elementary)
Helps students understand many of the economic, political, and social problems involved in dealing with pollution. Abt Associates.

Promotion (History, Social Studies, Problems of Democracy: Junior–Senior High)
Deals with the growth of cities, industries, the railroad, and mechanized agriculture to help students understand the complexity and interrelatedness of industrial and urban developments in late-nineteenth-century America. Science Research Associates.

Propaganda (Social Studies and Problems of Democracy: Upper Elementary–Senior High)
Designed to help students recognize propaganda in various techniques used by advertisers and others in trying to shape public opinion. Wff'n Proof.

Pursuit (History, Social Studies, and Problems of Democracy: Junior–Senior High)
Helps students understand how individual initiative, group effort, geographic location, and government action have been influential in furthering the cause of civil rights in the areas of education, housing, jobs, public accommodations, and voting since the 1950's. Educational Services, Reader's Digest, Inc., Pleasantville, N.Y. 10570.

Pythagoras (Mathematics: Elementary–Senior High)
Designed to help students learn spatial relations and understand geometric figures. Kohner Bros., Kohner Place, East Paterson, N.J. 07407.

Raid (Social Studies and Problems of Democracy: Junior–Senior High)

Designed to help disadvantaged students examine a variety of possible solutions to urban crime. Abt Associates.

Reconstruction (History: Junior–Senior High)
Students learn how social and political reform was difficult to achieve in the South after the Civil War because of the hostility and resistance among the governing classes of the South. Science Research Associates.

Revolution (History: Junior–Senior High)
Designed to help students understand the conflicts contributing to the development of the English Civil War. Two related simulations are *Adventuring* and *The English Civil War Unit*. Abt Associates.

Seal Hunting (Social Studies: Elementary)
Deals with the chance interaction of the worlds of seals and the Eskimo. Cf. *Bushman Exploring and Gathering*. Educational Development Center.

Section (Social Studies: Junior–Senior High)
Illustrates how economic and political interests influence the development of conflicts of interests among sections of a political territory. The Macmillan Company, School Division, 866 Third Ave., New York, N.Y. 10022.

Sierra Leone (Social Studies: Sixth Grade)
A computer-based game that requires the student to try to improve various aspects of the national economy. Abt Associates.

Star Power (Social Studies and Problems of Democracy: Junior High–Adult)
Students learn about the uses and abuses of power when the wealthiest group in the society makes all the rules. Western Behavioral Sciences Institute.

Steam (History: Junior–Senior High)
Illustrates the interrelationships of coal mining and steam engines in nineteenth-century England. Abt Associates.

Sumerian (Social Studies: Elementary)
A computer-based game that requires the student as ruler of an agricultural economy to try to improve his people's standard of living. Board of Cooperative Educational Services.

Sunshine (Social Studies and Problems of Democracy: Elementary–Senior High)
Students, simulating members of different racial groups in a mythical city, explore ways of dealing with a variety of urban problems. Interact.

Teeko (Mathematics: Upper Elementary–High School)
Students learn strategies in forming line segments and squares. John Scarne Games, Fairview, N.J. 07022

Wff'n Proof (Mathematics: Upper Elementary–High School)
Designed to help students grasp mathematical logic. Wff'n Proof.

Bibliography

1. Alexander, W. M., ed. *The High School of the Future: A Memorial to Kimball Wiles.* Columbus, Ohio: Charles E. Merrill, 1969.

2. American Civil Liberties Union. *Academic Freedom in the Secondary Schools.* New York: American Civil Liberties Union, 1963.

3. Association for Childhood Education International. *Feelings and Learning.* Washington, D.C.: Association for Childhood Education International, 1965.

4. Aylesworth, T. G., and Reagan, G. M. *Teaching for Thinking.* Garden City, N.Y.: Doubleday, 1969.

5. Backman, C. W., and Secord, P. F. *A Social Psychological View of Education.* New York: Harcourt Brace Jovanovich, 1968.

6. Barlow, J. "Game Simulation in U.S. History." In *Teaching Strategies and Classroom Realities,* edited by M. G. McClosky, pp. 201–6. Englewood Cliffs, N.J.: Prentice-Hall, 1971.

7. Berman, L. M. *New Priorities in the Curriculum.* Columbus, Ohio: Charles E. Merrill, 1968.

8. Bernard, H. W. *Human Development in Western Culture.* 3d ed. Boston: Allyn and Bacon, 1970.

9. Biehler, R. F. *Psychology Applied to Teaching.* Boston: Houghton Mifflin, 1971.

10. Blackie, J. *Inside the Primary School.* New York: Schocken Books, 1971.

11. Blishen, E., ed. *The School That I'd Like.* Baltimore, Md.: Penguin Books, 1969.

12. Bower, E. M., and Hollister, W. G., eds. *Behavioral Science Frontiers in Education.* New York: John Wiley & Sons, 1967.

13. Brameld, T. *Education for the Emerging Age.* New York: Harper & Row, 1965.

14. Brown, B. F. *The Appropriate Placement School: A Sophisticated Nongraded Curriculum.* New York: Parker Publishing Co., 1965.

15. Brown, B. F. *The Nongraded High School.* Englewood Cliffs, N.J.: Prentice-Hall, 1963.

16. Bruner, J. S. *The Process of Education.* Cambridge, Mass.: Harvard University Press, 1960.

17. Burton, W. H. *The Guidance of Learning Activities.* 3d ed. New York: Appleton-Century-Crofts, 1962.

18. Cantor, N. *The Teaching-Learning Process.* New York: Dryden Press, 1953.

19. Central Advisory Council for Education. *Children and Their Primary Schools,* 2 vols. London: Her Majesty's Stationery Office, 1967.

20. Channon, G. *Homework: Required Reading for Teachers and Parents.* New York: Outerbridge & Dienstfrey, 1970.

21. Charnofsky, S. *Educating the Powerless.* Belmont, Calif.: Wadsworth Publishing Co., 1971.

22. Chesler, M., and Fox, R. *Role-Playing Methods in the Classroom.* Chicago: Science Research Associates, 1966.

23. Coleman, J. S. *The Adolescent Society: The Social Life of the Teenager and Its Impact on Education.* New York: Free Press, 1961.

24. Combs, A. W. "Intelligence from a Perceptual Point of View." *Journal of Abnormal Social Psychology,* XLVII, No. 3 (1952), 662–73.

25. Combs, A. W., ed. *Perceiving, Behaving, Becoming: A New Focus for Education.* (1962 ASCD Yearbook.) Washington, D.C.: Association for Supervision and Curriculum Development, 1962.

26. Coopersmith, S. *The Antecedents of Self-Esteem.* San Francisco: W. H. Freeman, 1967.

27. Crary, R. W. *Humanizing the School: Curriculum Development and Theory.* New York: Alfred A. Knopf, 1969.

28. Cuban, L. *To Make a Difference: Teaching in the Inner City.* New York: Free Press, 1970.

29. Davis, D. C. *Model for a Humanistic Education: The Danish Folk Highschool.* Columbus, Ohio: Charles E. Merrill, 1971.

30. Davis, G. A., and Scott, J. A. *Training Creative Thinking.* New York: Holt, Rinehart & Winston, 1971.

31. Dennison, G. *The Lives of Children.* New York: Random House, 1969.

32. Dewey, J. *Democracy and Education.* New York: Macmillan, 1916.

33. Dewey, J. *Experience and Education.* New York: Macmillan, 1938.

34. Ebel, R. L., ed. *Encyclopedia of Educational Research.* 4th ed. New York: Macmillan, 1969.

35. Eisner, E. W. "Research in Creativity: Some Findings and Conceptions." *Childhood Education,* XXXIX (1963), 371–75.

36. Elkind, D. *A Sympathetic Understanding of the Child Six to Sixteen.* Boston: Allyn and Bacon, 1971.

37. Engelmann, S. *Preventing Failure in the Primary Grades.* Chicago: Science Research Associates, 1969.

38. Epstein, C. *Intergroup Relations for the Classroom Teacher.* Boston: Houghton Mifflin, 1968.

39. Fantini, M., and Weinstein, G. *The Disadvantaged: Challenge to Education.* New York: Harper & Row, 1968.

40. Fantini, M., and Young, M. A. *Designing Education for Tomorrow's Cities.* New York: Holt, Rinehart & Winston, 1970.

41. Featherstone, J. *Schools Where Children Learn.* New York: Liveright, 1971.

42. Fox, R.; Luszki, M. B.; and Schmuck, R. *Diagnosing Classroom Learning Environments.* Chicago: Science Research Associates, 1966.

43. Friebel, A. C. "Mathematical Instruction." In *Teaching the Disadvantaged Child,* edited by S. W. Tiedt, pp. 173–91. New York: Oxford University Press, 1968.

44. Friedenberg, E. Z. *Coming of Age in America.* New York: Random House, 1965.

45. Friedenberg, E. Z. *The Dignity of Youth and Other Atavisms.* Boston: Beacon Press, 1965.

46. Gage, N. L., ed. *Handbook of Research on Teaching.* Chicago: Rand McNally, 1963.

47. Gagné, R. M. *The Conditions of Learning.* 2d ed. New York: Holt, Rinehart & Winston, 1970.

48. Gagné, R. M. "Contributions of Learning to Human Development." *Psychological Review,* LXXV (1968), 177–91.

49. Gagné, R. M. "Educational Objectives and Human Performance." In *Learning and the Educational Process,* edited by J. D. Krumboltz, pp. 1–24. Chicago: Rand McNally, 1965.

50. Gagné, R. M. "Learning Hierarchies." *Educational Psychologist,* VI (1968), 1–8.

51. Gardner, J. W. *Excellence: Can We Be Equal and Excellent Too?* New York: Harper & Row, 1961.

52. Gattegno, C. *What We Owe Children.* New York: Outerbridge & Dienstfrey, 1970.

53. Getzels, J. W., and Jackson, P. W. "The Teacher's Personality and Characteristics." In *Handbook of Research on Teaching,* edited by N. L. Gage, pp. 506–82. Chicago: Rand McNally, 1963.

54. Ginott, H. *Between Parent and Child.* New York: Macmillan, 1965.

55. Ginott, H. *Between Parent and Teenager.* New York: Macmillan, 1969.

56. Ginsburg, H., and Opper, S. *Piaget's Theory of Intellectual Development: An Introduction.* Englewood Cliffs, N.J.: Prentice-Hall, 1969.

57. Glaser, R. "The Design of Instruction." In *The Changing American School,* edited by J. I. Goodlad (65th Yearbook, National Society for the Study of Education), Part II, pp. 215–42. Chicago: University of Chicago Press, 1966.

58. Glasser, W. *Schools Without Failure.* New York: Harper & Row, 1969.

59. Goodlad, J. I. "Meeting Children Where They Are." *Saturday Review,* March 20, 1965.

60. Goodlad, J. I. "The Schools vs. Education." *Saturday Review,* April 19, 1969.

61. Goodlad, J. I., and Anderson, R. H. *The Nongraded Elementary School.* Rev. ed. New York: Harcourt Brace Jovanovich, 1963.

62. Gordon, A. K. *Games for Growth.* Chicago: Science Research Associates, 1970.

63. Gordon, R., and Gordon, K. *The Blight on the Ivy.* Englewood Cliffs, N.J.: Prentice-Hall, 1963.

64. Gordon, T. *Parent Effectiveness Training.* New York: Peter H. Wyden, 1970.

65. Gorman, A. H. *Teachers and Learners: The Interactive Process of Education.* Boston: Allyn and Bacon, 1969.

66. Grambs, J. D. *Schools, Scholars and Society.* Englewood Cliffs, N.J.: Prentice-Hall, 1965.

67. Gross, B., and Gross, R. *Radical School Reform.* New York: Simon and Schuster, 1969.

68. Guskin, A. E., and Guskin, S. L. *A Social Psychology of Education.* Reading, Mass.: Addison-Wesley, 1970.

69. Hamachek, D. "Characteristics of Good Teachers and Implications for Teacher Education." *Phi Delta Kappan,* February 1969.

70. Hart, H. H., ed. *Summerhill: For and Against.* New York: Hart Publishing Co., 1970.

71. Hart, L. A. *The Classroom Disaster.* New York: Teachers College Press, 1969.

72. Hertzberg, A., and Stone, E. F. *Schools are for Children.* New York: Schocken Books, 1971.

73. Hilgard, E., ed. *Theories of Learning and Instruction* (63d Yearbook, National Society for the Study of Education), Part I. Chicago: University of Chicago Press, 1964.

74. Holt, J. *How Children Fail.* New York: Pitman, 1964.

75. Holt, J. *How Children Learn.* New York: Pitman, 1967.

76. Holt, J. *The Underachieving School.* New York: Pitman, 1969.

77. Holt, J. *What Do I Do Monday?* New York: E. P. Dutton, 1970.

78. Horrocks, J. E. *The Psychology of Adolescence: Behavior and Development.* 3d ed. Boston: Houghton Mifflin, 1969.

79. Howes, V. M. *Individualization of Instruction.* New York: Macmillan, 1970.

80. Howes, V. M. *Individualizing Instruction in Reading and Social Studies: Selected Readings on Programs and Practices.* New York: Macmillan, 1970.

81. Howes, V. M. *Individualizing Instruction in Science and Mathematics: Selected Readings on Programs, Practices, and Uses of Technology.* New York: Macmillan, 1970.

82. Hunt, J. McV. *Intelligence and Experience.* New York: Ronald Press, 1961.

83. Hunter, M. "Tailor Your Teaching to Individualized Instruction." *Instructor,* LXXIX, No. 7 (March 1970), 53–63.

84. Inhelder, B., and Piaget, J. *The Growth of Logical Thinking from Childhood to Adolescence.* New York: Basic Books, 1958.

85. Jackson, P. W. *Life in Classrooms.* New York: Holt, Rinehart & Winston, 1968.

86. Johnson, L. V., and Bany, M. A. *Classroom Management.* New York: Macmillan, 1970.

87. Kohl, H. R. *The Open Classroom.* New York: Random House, 1969.

88. Kohl, H. R. *36 Children.* New York: New American Library, 1967.

89. LaBenne, W. D., and Greene, B. I. *Educational Implications of Self-Concept Theory.* Pacific Palisades, Calif.: Goodyear Publishing Co., 1969.

90. Leacock, E. B. *Teaching and Learning in City Schools: A Comparative Study.* New York: Basic Books, 1969.

91. Lembo, J. M. *The Psychology of Effective Classroom Instruction.* Columbus, Ohio: Charles E. Merrill, 1969.

92. Lembo, J. M. *Why Teachers Fail.* Columbus, Ohio: Charles E. Merrill, 1971.

93. Lindberg, L. *The Democratic Classroom: A Guide for Teachers.* New York: Teachers College Press, 1954.

94. Lyon, H. C. *Learning to Feel—Feeling to Learn.* Columbus, Ohio: Charles E. Merrill, 1971.

95. McClosky, M. G., ed. *Teaching Strategies and Classroom Realities.* Englewood Cliffs, N.J.: Prentice-Hall, 1971.

96. McKeachie, W. J. *Teaching Tips: A Guidebook for the Beginning College Teacher.* Lexington, Mass.: D. C. Heath, 1969.

97. Maier, N. R. F. *Problem-Solving Discussions and Conferences: Leadership Methods and Skills.* New York: McGraw-Hill, 1963.

98. Maslow, A. H., ed. *Motivation and Personality.* 2d ed. New York: Harper & Row, 1970.

99. Massialas, B. G., and Cox, C. B. *Inquiry in Social Studies.* New York: McGraw-Hill, 1966.

100. Massialas, B. G., and Zevin, J. *Creative Encounters in the Classroom.* New York: John Wiley & Sons, 1967.

101. Masters, J. "Discipline Problems?" In *Teaching Strategies and Classroom Realities,* edited by M. G. McClosky, pp. 29–30. Englewood Cliffs, N.J.: Prentice-Hall, 1971.

102. Mathisen, B. "Games for Math." In *Teaching Strategies and Classroom Realities,* edited by M. G. McClosky, pp. 208–10. Englewood Cliffs, N.J.: Prentice-Hall, 1971.

103. Mayer, M. *Where, When, and Why: Social Studies in American Schools.* New York: Harper & Row, 1963.

104. Metcalf, L. E. "Research on Teaching the Social Studies." In *Handbook of Research on Teaching,* edited by N. L. Gage, pp. 929–65. Chicago: Rand McNally, 1963.

105. Miel, A., et al. *Cooperative Procedures in Learning.* New York: Teachers College Press, 1952.

106. Minuchin, P., et al. *The Psychological Impact of School Experience.* New York: Basic Books, 1969.

107. Montgomery County Student Alliance. "Wanted: A Humane Education: An Urgent Call for Reconciliation Between Rhetoric and Reality." In *Radical School Reform,* edited by R. Gross and B. Gross. New York: Simon & Schuster, 1969.

108. Morine, H., and Morine, G. *A Primer for the Inner-City School.* New York: McGraw-Hill, 1970.

109. Morse, W. C., and Wingo, G. M. *Psychology and Teaching.* 3d ed. Glenview, Ill.: Scott, Foresman & Co., 1969.

110. Mouly, G. J. *Psychology for Effective Teaching.* 2d ed. New York: Holt, Rinehart & Winston, 1968.

111. Murrow, C., and Murrow, L. *Children Come First: The Inspired Work of English Primary Schools.* New York: American Heritage Press, 1971.

112. National Education Association, Research Division. "Teacher Opinion Poll." *NEA Journal,* LII (December 1963), 34.

113. Neill, A. S. *Summerhill: A Radical Approach to Child Rearing.* New York: Hart Publishing Co., 1960.

114. Parker, J. C., and Rubin, L. J. *Process as Content: Curriculum Design and the Application of Knowledge.* Chicago: Rand McNally, 1966.

115. Parsons, C. *Schools Can Change.* Boston: Sterling Institute Press, 1969.

116. Perkins, H. V. *Human Development and Learning.* Belmont, Calif.: Wadsworth Publishing Co., 1969.

117. Piaget, J. *The Child's Conception of the World*. London: Routledge & Kegan Paul, 1929.

118. Piaget, J. *Judgment and Reasoning in the Child*. New York: Harcourt Brace Jovanovich, 1928.

119. Piaget, J. *Language and Thought of the Child*. London: Routledge & Kegan Paul, 1926.

120. Piaget, J. *The Psychology of Intelligence*. New York: Harcourt Brace Jovanovich, 1950.

121. Postman, N., and Weingartner, C. *The Soft Revolution*. New York: Delacorte, 1971.

122. Postman, N., and Weingartner, C. *Teaching as a Subversive Activity*. New York: Delacorte, 1969.

123. Purkey, W. W. *Self-Concept and School Achievement*. Englewood Cliffs, N.J.: Prentice-Hall, 1970.

124. Rasmussen, M., ed. *Readings from Childhood Education: Articles of Lasting Value*. Washington, D.C.: Association for Childhood Education International, 1966.

125. Raths, L. E.; Harmin, M.; and Simon, S. B. *Values and Teaching: Working with Values in the Classroom*. Columbus, Ohio: Charles E. Merrill, 1966.

126. Redl, F. *When We Deal with Children*. New York: Free Press, 1966.

127. Renfield, R. *If Teachers Were Free*. Washington, D.C.: Acropolis, 1969.

128. Repo, S., ed. *This Book Is About Schools*. New York: Pantheon Books, 1970.

129. Rhea, B. "Institutional Paternalism in High Schools." *The Urban Review*, II, No. 4 (1968), 13–15.

130. Rich, J. M. *Education and Human Values*. Reading, Mass.: Addison-Wesley, 1968.

131. Riessman, F. *The Culturally Deprived Child*. New York: Harper & Row, 1962.

132. Riessman, F. *Hip Word Game Workbook*. Chicago: Follett, 1967.

133. Riessman, F. "Styles of Learning." *NEA Journal*, LV, No. 3 (March 1966), 15–17.

134. Ripple, R., and Rockcastle, N. *Piaget Rediscovered*. (A Report of the Conference on Cognitive Studies and Curriculum Development.) Ithaca, N.Y.: School of Education, Cornell University, 1964.

135. Rogers, C. R. *Freedom to Learn.* Columbus, Ohio: Charles E. Merrill, 1969.

136. Rogers, C. R. *On Becoming a Person.* Boston: Houghton Mifflin, 1961.

137. Rogers, V. *Teaching in the British Primary Schools.* New York: Macmillan, 1970.

138. Rosenthal, R., and Jacobson, L. *Pygmalion in the Classroom.* New York: Holt, Rinehart & Winston, 1968.

139. Rosenthal, R., and Jacobson, L. "Teacher Expectations for the Disadvantaged." *Scientific American,* CCXVIII, No. 4 (1968).

140. Schaefer, R. J. *The School as a Center of Inquiry.* New York: Harper & Row, 1967.

141. Schmuck, R; Chesler, M.; and Lippitt, R. *Problem Solving to Improve Classroom Learning.* Chicago: Science Research Associates, 1966.

142. Schreiber, D., ed. *Profile of the School Dropout.* New York: Random House, 1968.

143. Selakovich, D. *Social Studies for the Disadvantaged.* New York: Holt, Rinehart & Winston, 1970.

144. Sigel, I. E.; Roeper, A.; and Hooper, F. H. "A Training Procedure for Acquisition of Piaget's Conservation of Quantity." *British Journal of Educational Psychology,* XXXVI (1966), 301–11.

145. Silberman, C. *Crisis in the Classroom.* New York: Random House, 1970.

146. Silberman, M. L., ed. *The Experience of Schooling.* New York: Holt, Rinehart & Winston, 1971.

147. Skeel, D. J. *Children of the Street: Teaching in the Inner City.* Pacific Palisades, Calif.: Goodyear Publishing Co., 1971.

148. Skeel, D. J., and Hagen, O. A. *The Process of Curriculum Change.* Pacific Palisades, Calif.: Goodyear Publishing Co., 1971.

149. Skinner, B. F. *The Technology of Teaching.* New York: Appleton-Century-Crofts, 1968.

150. Smith, H. P. *Psychology in Teaching.* 2d ed. Englewood Cliffs, N.J.: Prentice-Hall, 1962.

151. Smith, L. M., and Geoffrey, W. *The Complexities of an Urban Classroom: An Analysis Toward a General Theory of Teaching.* New York: Holt, Rinehart & Winston, 1968.

152. Sprinthall, R. C., and Sprinthall, N. A., eds. *Educational Psychology: Selected Readings.* New York: Van Nostrand-Reinhold, 1969.

153. Stanford, G., and Stanford, B. D. *Learning Discussion Skills Through Games.* New York: Citation Press, 1969.

154. Stone, J. C., and Schneider, F. W., eds. *Teaching in the Inner City: A Book of Readings.* New York: Thomas Y. Crowell, 1970.

155. Stone, L. J., and Church, J. *Childhood and Adolescence.* 2d ed. New York: Random House, 1968.

156. Strom, R. D. *Psychology for the Classroom.* Englewood Cliffs, N.J.: Prentice-Hall, 1969.

157. Strom, R. D., ed. *Teachers and the Learning Process.* Englewood Cliffs, N.J.: Prentice-Hall, 1971.

158. Suchman, J. R. *The Elementary School Training Program in Scientific Inquiry.* Urbana, Ill.: University of Illinois Press, 1962.

159. Suchman, J. R. "Inquiry Training: Building Skills for Autonomous Discovery." *Merrill-Palmer Quarterly,* VII, No. 3 (1961), 147–71.

160. Taba, H. "Teaching Strategies and Thought Processes." *Teachers College Record,* LXV (1964), 524–34.

161. Tanner, L. N., and Lindgren, H. C. *Classroom Teaching and Learning: A Mental Health Approach.* New York: Holt, Rinehart & Winston, 1971.

162. Thatcher, M. D. "Popular Songs and Poetry." In *Teaching Strategies and Classroom Realities,* edited by M. G. McClosky, pp. 235–36. Englewood Cliffs, N.J.: Prentice-Hall, 1971.

163. Tiedt, S. W., ed. *Teaching the Disadvantaged Child.* New York: Oxford University Press, 1968.

164. Torrance, E. P. *Encouraging Creativity in the Classroom.* Dubuque, Iowa: Wm. C. Brown Co., 1970.

165. Von Hilsheimer, G. *How to Live with Your Special Child: A Handbook for Behavior Change.* Washington, D.C.: Acropolis, 1970.

166. Waskin, Y., and Parrish, L. *Teacher-Pupil Planning for Better Classroom Learning.* New York: Pitman, 1967.

167. Weinstein, G., and Fantini, M., eds. *Toward Humanistic Education: A Curriculum of Affect.* New York: Praeger, 1970.

168. *West Virginia Board of Education* v. *Barnette,* 319 U.S. 624 (1943).

169. White, M. A. "The View from the Pupil's Desk." *The Urban Review,* II, No. 5 (April 1968), 5–7.

170. White, R. K., and Lippitt, R. O. *Autocracy and Democracy.* New York: Harper & Row, 1960.
171. White, R. W. "Motivation Reconsidered: The Concept of Competence." *Psychological Review,* LXVI (1959), 297–333.
172. Wilson, L. C. *The Open Access Curriculum.* Boston: Allyn and Bacon, 1971.
173. Withall, J., and Lewis, W. W. "Social Interaction in the Classroom." In *Handbook of Research on Teaching,* edited by N. L. Gage, pp. 683–714. Chicago: Rand McNally, 1963.
174. Zimbardo, P., and Ebbesen, E. B. *Influencing Attitudes and Changing Behavior: A Basic Introduction to Relevant Methodology, Theory, and Applications.* Reading, Mass.: Addison-Wesley, 1969.

Index